C0-AWU-595

By GRACE

and Other Sermons

by
Oliver B. Greene

The Gospel Hour, Inc., Oliver B. Greene, Director
Box 2024, Greenville, South Carolina 29602

© Copyright 1970 by Oliver B. Greene
All rights reserved
Printed in the United States of America

First printing, July 1970 — 15,000 copies

$5.00

FOREWORD

The compilation of the sermons in this book was prompted by a desire to help God's people grasp a better understanding of the riches of God's grace. Many believers are spiritual paupers because they do not realize that through the provision of God's grace the abundance of heaven's storehouse is at their disposal.

The Apostle Paul, God's minister to the Church, speaks freely of "the *unsearchable riches* of Christ" (Eph. 3:8), the riches of God's "goodness and forbearance and longsuffering" (Rom. 2:4), and tells us that God grants "the *forgiveness of sins* according to the riches of His grace" (Eph. 1:7). Then in Philippians 4:19 he tells us, "My God shall supply all your need *according to his riches in glory BY CHRIST JESUS!*"

We can never fully understand the grace of God nor the scope of His great love for a sinful world. But it is the prayer of the author that through the reading of these pages Christians may be enriched in the knowledge of the riches we possess in Christ, and that unbelievers may come to see the beauty and worth of surrendering all to Him.

—*The Author*

Contents

BY GRACE

By Grace

"For BY GRACE are ye saved through faith; and that not of yourselves: it is the gift of God: not of works, lest any man should boast" (Eph. 2:8, 9).

"Salvation is of the Lord" (Jonah 2:9), therefore salvation is *by GRACE*—all of grace. "And if by grace, then is it no more of works" (Rom. 11:6).

The age-old definition of grace is simply *"God's unmerited favor toward man."* But when we read the account of the sufferings of Jesus as foretold by the prophets and in the Psalms (and fulfilled in the Gospels) we realize that we can give *a very limited* definition of grace. Quoting from Titus 3:4, 5 we can define grace as "the kindness and love of God our Saviour toward man . . . not by works of righteousness which we have done."

In the Scriptures, grace is constantly set in contrast to the Law of Moses. Under the Law of Moses, God demanded righteousness *from man;* but under grace, God in Christ *gives* righteousness *TO man.*

In John 1:17 we read, "The law was given by Moses, *but GRACE and TRUTH came by Jesus Christ."* The law was connected with Moses and with works, but *grace* came by Jesus Christ—yea, *grace IS Jesus Christ*—and becomes ours by faith. The law extended blessings to the good, but *grace* extends *salvation* to the *bad!* Grace provides for us that which we do not deserve. Therefore I maintain that the Bible teaches grace as being *OF God, THROUGH God, ALL of God—the GIFT of God to an undeserving world*, and God's grace is all-sufficient. The believer is in Christ, and we are *COMPLETE in Him* (Col. 2:10).

In this message I want us to study the *"ALL THINGS"* that are ours in Christ, ours by grace. God's delight is in the sinner made a saint *BY GRACE through FAITH in Jesus, the Son.* Therefore *ALL THINGS are ours, for we are Christ's, and Christ is God's* (I Cor. 3:21-23).

All Spiritual Blessings

"Blessed be the God and Father of our Lord Jesus Christ, who hath blessed us with ALL SPIRITUAL BLESSINGS in heavenly places in Christ" (Eph. 1:3).

Here is set forth the totality of God's bestowment in Christ Jesus. All spiritual blessings are to be found *in the Lord Jesus*, all spiritual blessings come to us *through* the Lord Jesus, "for in Him dwelleth all the fulness of the Godhead bodily, *and ye are complete IN HIM*, which is the head of all principality and power" (Col. 2:9, 10). That leaves *man* out of it! The only Man who ever completely pleased God was the Man Christ Jesus, and the only way you and I can please God is through His Son.

Since all spiritual blessings come by and through Christ, it becomes clear that our *salvation* comes through Christ. He declared, *"I am THE Way"* (John 14:6), and there is *no other* way! He also declared, "I am *THE Door"* (John 10:9). There is no other entrance to heaven. "Whosoever shall call upon *the name of the Lord* shall be saved" (Rom. 10:13). Notice—not whosoever shall call upon the name of the Virgin Mary, or the name of the priest, or the name of some preacher, but whosoever shall call upon *the name of the LORD.* "Neither is there salvation in any other: for there is *none other name* under heaven given among men, whereby we must be saved" (Acts 4:12).

All spiritual blessings come by Christ. Therefore He is our salvation, our victory, our sanctification, and in Him we find reward for our labors. In I Corinthians 1:30, 31 the Holy Spirit declared through the pen of Paul, "Of (God) are ye in Christ Jesus, who of God is made unto us *wisdom,* and *righteousness,* and *sanctification,* and *redemption:* that, according as it is written, He that glorieth, let him glory in the Lord!"

Looking at these verses more closely we see that there must be wisdom and understanding before there can be true conversion—and *Christ is* our wisdom. All our righteousnesses are as "filthy

11

rags" (Isa. 64:6), therefore we must find righteousness in someone other than ourselves; so *Christ the Righteous One* becomes *our* righteousness. We have not within ourselves the ability to live sanctified lives (Rom. 7:18), therefore *Christ* is our *sanctification*. Unregenerate man is by nature a child of wrath, a child of the devil (Eph. 2:3); but Christ is our redemption.

You see, Jesus left the Father's bosom and came into this world in a body of flesh. Through His life, death, and resurrection He accomplished the following:

He bruised the serpent's head (Gen. 3:15).

He overcame the world (John 16:33).

He destroyed the works of the devil (I John 3:8).

He removed the fear of death (Heb. 2:9-15).

He spoiled principalities and powers (Col. 2:15).

He now holds the keys of hell and of death (Rev. 1:18).

Is it any wonder that God blesses us with *"all spiritual blessings"* in Christ Jesus?

All Wisdom

"In whom we have redemption through His blood, the forgiveness of sins, according to the riches of His grace; wherein He hath abounded toward us in ALL WISDOM and prudence" (Eph. 1:7, 8).

ALL wisdom is revealed in the giving of God's love "according to the riches of His grace." The wisdom of man is foolishness to God. In spite of the fact that man in his thinking has tried to outlaw and bypass God, no man can have rest in his mind or peace in his heart until he is in the right relationship with God—and no man can be in the right relationship with God until he knows God's Son as personal Saviour. The wisdom of God conceived, perfected, and provided the wonderful plan of salvation, and the Son of God brought that salvation down to you and to me—to any and all who, by faith, accept His finished work.

"The fear of the Lord is the beginning of knowledge" (Prov. 1:7). When we fear God, and as a result of godly fear we receive His Son as our Saviour, Christ is then *made unto us WISDOM*. Thus when we are born again we have the mind of Christ and the wisdom of God abiding within us. All the wisdom of the eternal Godhead is wrapped up in our Christ:

We are saved by His marvelous grace (Eph. 2:8).

We are led by His precious Spirit (Rom. 8:14).

We are sealed by His Spirit until the day of redemption (Eph. 4:30).

We are kept by His wonderful power (Rom. 8:38, 39; I Pet. 1:5).

All that I need I find in Jesus, and I am willing to follow as He leads. I am willing for Him to choose for me, and I am trusting all the days of my future into His hands. I can say with the

Psalmist, "Surely goodness and mercy shall follow me all the days of my life: and I will dwell in the house of the Lord for ever!" (Psalm 23:6).

All Things In Christ

"That in the dispensation of the fulness of times He might gather together in one ALL THINGS IN CHRIST, both which are in heaven, and which are on earth, even in Him" (Eph. 1:10).

Regardless of the sad state of affairs in this earth today, at the appointed time God's Christ will bring order out of chaos. Because of Adam's sin, the whole creation groans and travails in pain (Rom. 8:22). Genesis 3:14-19 tells the sad story:

"And the Lord God said unto the serpent, Because thou hast done this, thou art cursed above all cattle, and above every beast of the field. Upon thy belly shalt thou go, and dust shalt thou eat all the days of thy life: and I will put enmity between thee and the woman, and between thy seed and her seed; it shall bruise thy head, and thou shalt bruise His heel.

"Unto the woman He said, I will greatly multiply thy sorrow and thy conception. In sorrow thou shalt bring forth children; and thy desire shall be to thy husband, and he shall rule over thee.

"And unto Adam He said, Because thou hast hearkened unto the voice of thy wife, and hast eaten of the tree, of which I commanded thee, saying, Thou shalt not eat of it: cursed is the

14

ground for thy sake; in sorrow shalt thou eat of it all the days of thy life. Thorns also and thistles shall it bring forth to thee; and thou shalt eat the herb of the field. In the sweat of thy face shalt thou eat bread, till thou return unto the ground; for out of it wast thou taken: for dust thou art, and unto dust shalt thou return."

There would never have been a thorn or a thistle; there would never have been bloodshed, pain, or sorrow—if Adam had not sinned! The first Adam sold us into wholesale sin and death; but thank God, the last Adam, the Lord Jesus Christ, bought us back through the tremendous price of His precious blood:

"For if by one man's offence death reigned by one; much more they which receive abundance of grace and of the gift of righteousness shall reign in life by One, Jesus Christ. Therefore as by the offence of one judgment came upon all men to condemnation; even so by the righteousness of One the free gift came upon all men unto justification of life. For as by one man's disobedience many were made sinners, so by the obedience of One shall many be made righteous. Moreover the law entered, that the offence might abound. But where sin abounded, grace did much more abound: that as sin hath reigned unto death, even so might grace reign through righteousness unto eternal life by Jesus Christ our Lord" (Rom. 5:17-21).

Jesus came the first time for the purpose of

paying the penalty for our sin. He paid that tremendous debt in full, and because of His sacrifice of Himself we have salvation for our souls. But He is coming again for the purpose of redeeming our bodies, that we might be like Him (I John 3:2). He will "change our vile body, that it may be fashioned like unto His glorious body, according to the working whereby He is able even to subdue all things unto Himself" (Phil. 3:21). When Jesus comes the second time He will deliver the whole creation from the curse (Rom. 8:18-23; Isa. ch. 11) *and "there shall BE no more curse"* (Rev. 22:3).

When Jesus gathers all things unto Himself this earth will be a grand and glorious Paradise. There will be no thorns on the roses, no weeds in the gardens, no thistles to mar the beauty of the hillsides of God's creation. For mankind there will be no sin, sorrow, pain, heartache, or disappointment. There will be no sickness or death. Even the animal kingdom will be as it was in the first Paradise when Adam named the animals as God caused them to pass by (Gen. 2:19, 20). They shall not hurt nor destroy in all of God's holy mountain, for the earth will then be filled with the knowledge of the Lord as the waters now cover the sea (Isa. 11:9). We hear *much talk* about peace. Men plan and strive to bring about "lasting" peace. But there will not be peace on earth and good will among men until Jesus sits on the throne of David in Jerusalem.

In Psalm 72 we find seven characteristics of Christ's kingdom when He sets up His rule on earth and all things are gathered unto Him:

1. His kingdom will be *righteous in its rule:*

"He shall judge thy people with righteousness, and thy poor with judgment" (Psalm 72:2). The Righteous Judge will do the right thing *because* it is right. Crooked men make crooked government; but in that glad day "the government shall be upon *His* shoulder" (Isa. 9:6), and He will rule in righteousness *because He IS righteous.*

2. His government will be *saving in its strength:*

"He shall judge the poor of the people, He shall save the children of the needy, and shall break in pieces the oppressor" (Psalm 72:4). As bread saves the needy from starvation and as the strong man delivers the weak from the oppressor, even so will Jesus vindicate all who are needy and oppressed. There will be no oppression and no want in His glorious kingdom.

3. His kingdom will provide *blessing in its bestowment:*

"He shall come down like rain upon the mown grass: as showers that water the earth" (Psalm 72:6). As the rains soften the hard ground and germinate the seeds, causing them to sprout and bring forth fruit, even so Christ will bless all who dwell in His kingdom.

4. His kingdom will be *universal in its scope:*

"He shall have dominion also from sea to sea,

and from the river unto the ends of the earth"
(Psalm 72:8). Down through recorded centuries,
men have tried to conquer and enslave earth's
billions, but in vain! They may conquer and rule
for a season, but eventually the conquerors are
themselves vanquished by another stronger than
they. There will be none to conquer Him who is
to come, the Righteous One who will rule from the
throne of David and of whose kingdom there shall
be no end.

5. His kingdom shall be *succoring in its help:*
"For He shall deliver the needy when he crieth,
the poor also, and him that hath no helper" (Psalm
72:12). There will be no poor or needy people in
Christ's kingdom. There will be no hunger, no
deprivation, and no lack of love, for the heart of
the King will be as tender as that of a mother toward her newborn babe! Think of the poor, lonely,
hungry, heartsick millions on earth today. Such
conditions will not be known when Jesus gathers
all things unto Himself.

6. His kingdom will be *redemptive in its exercise:*
"He shall redeem their soul from deceit and violence: and precious shall their blood be in His
sight" (Psalm 72:14). The reign of Jesus on earth
will be free from all sin and sin's attendant evils.
Nothing will enter there to defile, and righteousness will cover the earth.

7. His kingdom shall be *forever:*
"His name shall endure for ever: His name

shall be continued as long as the sun: and men shall be blessed in Him: all nations shall call Him blessed" (Psalm 72:17). The ills of this old, sin-sick, weary world call for the coming of the King of Righteousness with healing in His wings! Earth's ills will never be cured until He comes in right-eousness to gather all things unto Himself. There-fore I pray with John the Beloved, "Even so, come, Lord Jesus!" (Rev. 22:20).

All Things After the Counsel of God's Will

"In whom also we have obtained an inheritance, being predestinated according to the purpose of Him who worketh ALL THINGS AFTER THE COUNSEL OF HIS OWN WILL" (Eph. 1:11).

God has a plan, a program, a blueprint for the ages, and He is working out that plan and program according to the counsel of His own will. He has a predestined plan for His children, and all hell cannot change that plan. The devil is mighty, but God is almighty. It is God's good pleasure to give the kingdom to His children, and all things which have to do with the children of God will be worked out as planned in the beginning.

In the Garden of Eden the devil tried to steal the soul of man, but God cursed the serpent and promised the Deliverer (Gen. 3:15). In "the fulness of the time" the Deliverer came (Gal. 4:4), and thus was thwarted the devil's plan to damn all mankind. True, he has damned the souls of many;

but many, many others have believed on the Lord Jesus Christ unto glorious salvation.

When the devil met Jesus on the Mount of Temptation he tried to tie up the kingdoms of the earth for himself. He tried to entice Jesus to sell out to him. He "sheweth Him all the kingdoms of the world, and the glory of them; and saith unto Him: *All these things will I give thee, if thou wilt fall down and worship me!*" That was Satan's subtle attempt to gain control of the earth forever—but he failed. Jesus answered, "Get thee hence, Satan: for it is written, Thou shalt worship the Lord thy God, and Him only shalt thou serve" (Matt. 4:8-10). It is true that the devil has temporary control over the world. He is "the god of this age" (II Cor. 4:4), "the prince of the power of the air" (Eph. 2:2); but he is a defeated foe and at the appointed time in God's program Jesus will personally supervise the binding of Satan, and will consign him to the bottomless pit forever (Rev. 20:10).

In the closing days of this Age of Grace the devil is trying mightily to destroy the Church. He is using every subtle and devious plan his evil mind can conceive in his efforts to destroy the body of Christ, but all his efforts will ultimately fail. It is true that many local assemblies have sold out to the devil, but neither liberalists, modernists, nor "the gates of hell" can prevail against the Church of the living God (Matt. 16:18).

Love Unto All the Saints

"Wherefore I also, after I heard of your faith in the Lord Jesus, and LOVE UNTO ALL THE SAINTS, cease not to give thanks for you, making mention of you in my prayers" (Eph. 1:15, 16).

All the saints are in the *plan* of God, all the saints are in the *love* of God, and I thank God for saints who can *love one another!* I wonder how the dear Lord Jesus Christ feels today when He looks down from glory and sees the divisions that exist between believers—yes, even among those who claim to be fundamentalists, following the Word of God to the letter. Self-righteousness, pride, selfishness, a desire for personal gain and prestige quench the Spirit and hinder the influence of the Church. Denominational differences also bring about disagreement among God's people. Religious dictatorship and man-made programs have certainly hindered the progress of the Church. Preachers are not to be "lords over God's heritage, but . . . ensamples to the flock" (I Pet. 5:3). They are not to dictate to God's people, but rather lead them into the green pastures of His marvelous grace.

Born again Baptists should love born again Methodists, and vice versa. Born again Baptists and Methodists should love all other born again people. We may not agree on all points of doctrine, we may not do things in exactly the same way in our different local churches; but if "we be brethren" (Gen. 13:8), then we should be able to agree on the major doctrines even though we may disagree on the minor. The world watches Christians and appraises God by the lives we live before them. Therefore we cannot afford to fuss, fight, argue, and quibble with each other. If God's believing children would unite their hearts in prayer and combine their efforts in brotherly love in the interest of lost souls, this world would experience such revival as has never before been known! God's Word declares, "If a man say, *I love God,* and hateth his brother, he is a liar: for he that loveth not his brother whom he hath *seen,* how can he love God whom he *hath not* seen?" (I John 4:20).

The Holy Spirit dictated these precious words to the Apostle Paul and he penned them down for our instruction:

"For as the body is one, and hath many members, and all the members of that one body, being many, are one body: so also is Christ. For by one Spirit are we all baptized into one body, whether we be Jews or Gentiles, whether we be bond or free; and have been all made to drink into one Spirit. For the body is not one member, but many" (I Cor. 12:12-14).

That settles all argument! All saved people are members of the same body—the body of Christ (Eph. 5:30), which is the true Church. Whether you are Baptist, Methodist, Holiness, Presbyterian

—whatever denominational name you bear—if you are washed in the blood of Jesus you are a member of His body and you have been baptized into the New Testament Church. May God help us to stop splitting hairs over denominational differences while the world lies in darkness and despair, while untold millions are plunging wholesale into hell without Christ! He commanded the Church to carry the Gospel to the ends of the earth, making disciples of all men and teaching them to observe *all things which He had commanded* (Matt. 28:20)—not all things which different "religions" teach.

"God is love" (I John 4:8). Love is the essence of God, and love is the fruit of salvation. We who are saved are "saints" by the grace of God and we should love all other saints. Jesus said that the greatest commandment of all is to "love the Lord thy God with all thy heart, and with all thy soul, and with all thy mind. . . . And the second is like unto it: Thou shalt love thy neighbour as thyself" (Matt. 22:37, 39). One of the outstanding needs among God's people today is a revival which will make us love one another as we should; for when we have love for the brethren as taught in the Word of God, the divisions in the churches will automatically disappear. All saints are in the plan of God's love and in the purpose of His saving grace.

All Principality, Power, Might, and Dominion

"*. . . that ye may know . . . what is the exceed-*

ing greatness of His power to us-ward who believe, according to the working of His mighty power, which He wrought in Christ, when He raised Him from the dead, and set Him at His own right hand in the heavenly places, far above ALL PRINCIPALITY, and POWER, and MIGHT, and DOMINION, and EVERY NAME that is named, not only in this world, but also in that which is to come: and hath put all things under His feet, and gave Him to be the head over all things to the Church, which is His body, the fulness of Him that filleth all in all" (Eph. 1:18-23).

What a declaration of the power of the Lord Jesus Christ—and *He lives in the heart* of every born again believer! All principality, and power, and might, and dominion are given to Christ, He is above all, and all things in heaven and in earth are under His feet. That makes me very happy! There is no power on earth or in heaven greater than the power of our Christ, therefore godless, atheistic dictators can demonstrate no more power than He is *willing* for them to demonstrate.

Our Christ is the God of the Old Testament. Through His power Nebuchadnezzar was driven from his throne (Dan. 4:4-37), the mighty King Belshazzar was slain (Dan. ch. 5)—and He was present when God cast Lucifer out of heaven (Luke 10:18). In John 16:33 Jesus said to His disciples, "In the world ye shall have tribulation: but be of good cheer. *I have overcome the world!"* So while the devil and his demons are powerful, God's Christ is *ALL-powerful* and we are more than conquerors *through Him!* (Rom. 8:31-39). "Ye are of God, little children, and have overcome them: because greater is He that is in you, than he that is in the world" (I John 4:4).

Jesus pleased the Father in all things (Matt. 3:17; 17:5; John 12:28), and the only possible way in which *you and I* can please God the Father is through Christ the Son. If we know the Son, we also know the Father (John 14:7-9; I John 2:23). If we confess the Son, He will confess us to the Father; but if we confess not the Son, He will not confess us to the heavenly Father (Matt. 10: 32, 33).

Is it any wonder God gave Christ to be *"the HEAD over ALL THINGS to the Church . . . the fulness of Him that filleth ALL IN ALL"?* Here is proclaimed the compass of His fulness. The Psalmist declared, "If I ascend up into heaven, thou art there. If I make my bed in hell, behold, thou art there. If I take the wings of the morning, and dwell in the uttermost parts of the sea, even there shall thy hand lead me, and thy right hand shall hold me" (Psalm 139:8-10). Revelation 21:23 tells us that in the New Jerusalem, the Lamb will be the light of the city. Hallelujah! What a Saviour! Is He *your* Saviour? If not, let Him save you now. If you are saved, then bow your head and worship Him for His wonderful salvation!

We All Were Children of Wrath

"And you hath He quickened, who were dead in trespasses and sins: wherein in time past ye walked according to the course of this world, according to the prince of the power of the air, the spirit that now worketh in the children of disobedience: among whom also WE ALL had our conversation in times past in the lusts of our flesh, fulfilling the desires of the flesh and of the mind; and were by nature THE CHILDREN OF WRATH, even as others" (Eph. 2:1-3).

These verses describe our condition before we were saved, so let us examine them more closely:

We were "dead in trespasses and sins."

We walked "according to the course of this world."

We walked "according to the prince of the power of the air" — and *the prince of the power of the air* is the devil.

We had the spirit of the children of disobedience.

We had our conversation "in the lusts of the flesh."

We fulfilled "the desires of the flesh and of the mind."

We were *"by nature* the children of wrath" — children of the devil.

Please notice, beloved, this description is not

26

applied to *some* of us, it is not applied to just the worst among us. It applies to *ALL of us* before we were saved! The only person fit for the kingdom of God is the person who has been cleansed by the blood of the Lord Jesus Christ. Even the best, most upright, most morally strict member of the human race is miserably lost if he (or she) does not have Jesus! Good works, righteous deeds, right living, sacrificial giving—yes, the very best we have to offer, is no better than filthy rags in the eyes of a holy God (Isa. 64:6).

In Romans chapter 3 Paul declared, ". . . we have before proved both Jews and Gentiles, that they are all under sin. As it is written, There is none righteous, no, not one: there is none that understandeth, there is none that seeketh after God. They are all gone out of the way, they are together become unprofitable; there is none that doeth good, no, not one.

"Their throat is an open sepulchre; with their tongues they have used deceit; the poison of asps is under their lips: whose mouth is full of cursing and bitterness. Their feet are swift to shed blood. Destruction and misery are in their ways, and the way of peace have they not known. There is no fear of God before their eyes. . . . *For ALL have sinned,* and come short of the glory of God" (Rom. 3:9-18, 23).

Yes, we were *ALL in the same condition*—dead in sin, undone, unrighteous, children of the devil, living in the lust of the flesh, enemies of God, without Christ and without hope! *"BUT GOD"*—here is where the hope of the soul begins—*"who is RICH IN MERCY, for His GREAT LOVE wherewith He loved us, even when we were dead in sins, hath quickened us together WITH CHRIST,* (by grace ye are saved;) *and hath raised us up together, and made us sit together in heavenly places in Christ Jesus"* (Eph. 2:4-6).

Here we see three things pertaining to our God:

He is *rich in mercy.*

He is *great in love.*

He has *life-giving power*—the power by which He quickened us (made us alive) when we were dead in sins, and "made us sit together in heavenly places in Christ Jesus."

Without God's mercy, every member of the human race would go to hell. We *deserve* damnation, and apart from God's mercy not one of us could miss the regions of the damned! It is only through the mercy of God that we can be made new creatures in Christ Jesus.

"Not by works of righteousness which we have done, but according to His MERCY He saved us, by the washing of regeneration, and renewing of the Holy Ghost" (Tit. 3:5). Dear soul, never rush into God's presence and demand *justice!* Rather, *plead His MERCY*, for if He should mete out *justice*, every soul would burn in hell! God's Word

decrees, *"The soul that SINNETH, it shall DIE"*
(Ezek. 18:4). The holiness of God declares, *"When
I see the BLOOD, I will pass over you"* (Ex. 12:13),
and Hebrews 9:22 tells us, *"WITHOUT shedding
of blood is no remission!"*

All—*yes, ALL*—Gentiles, Jews, rich, poor, wise,
unwise, bond, free, elite or scum-bum—are lost
without Christ, and apart from His shed blood
there is no remission of sins!

All the Building Fitly Framed Together

*"Now therefore ye are no more strangers and
foreigners, but fellowcitizens with the saints, and
of the household of God; and are built upon the
foundation of the apostles and prophets, Jesus
Christ Himself being the chief corner stone; in
whom ALL THE BUILDING FITLY FRAMED
TOGETHER groweth unto an holy temple in the
Lord"* (Eph. 2:19-21).

Before we were saved we were "without Christ,
. . . aliens from the commonwealth of Israel, . . .
strangers from the covenants of promise, having
no hope, and without God in the world. *BUT
NOW in Christ Jesus (we) who sometimes were far
off are made nigh BY THE BLOOD OF CHRIST"*
(Eph. 2:12, 13).

All unbelievers are dead in trespasses and sins—
yes, dead even while they live (Eph. 2:1; I Tim.
5:6).

All believers are alive unto God—alive in Christ

(Rom. 6:8-11), and all believers are members of the same glorious body:

"For as the body is one, and hath many members, and all the members of that one body, being many, are one body: *so also is CHRIST.* For by one Spirit are we *all baptized into one body,* whether we be Jews or Gentiles, whether we be bond or free; and have been all made to drink into one Spirit" (I Cor. 12:12, 13).

In the Church of the living God "there is neither Jew nor Greek, there is neither bond nor free, there is neither male nor female: *for ye are ALL ONE in Christ Jesus"* (Gal. 3:28).

"For HE is our peace, who hath made both one, and hath broken down the middle wall of partition between us; having abolished in His flesh the enmity, even the law of commandments contained in ordinances; for *to make in Himself of twain one new man,* so making peace; and that He might reconcile both unto God *in ONE BODY* by the cross, having slain the enmity thereby: and came and preached peace to you which were afar off, and to them that were nigh. *For THROUGH HIM we both have access by ONE SPIRIT unto the Father"* (Eph. 2:14-18).

Jesus broke down the middle wall of partition. He destroyed the enmity between God and man. He so loved *the world* — not just a few people, not just a select group or race, but the whole world — that He died for the entire human race. *He died for ALL* in order that *ALL who will come to God by Him* might become the children of God, "builded together for an habitation of God through the Spirit" (Eph. 2:22).

What happens the very moment we are saved?

We become possessors of divine nature (II Pet. 1:4).

We become possessors of the Holy Spirit (Rom. 8:9).

We become the temple of the Holy Spirit (I Cor. 6:19, 20).

We are sealed by the Holy Spirit (Eph. 4:30).

We become sons of God (I John 3:2).

We become heirs of God, joint-heirs with Jesus Christ (Rom. 8:17).

We are baptized into the body of Christ (I Cor. 12:12, 13).

We become citizens of heaven "from whence we look for the Saviour" (Phil. 3:20).

Yes, saved people are the habitation of God, for God lives in us. We are citizens of another world, strangers and pilgrims on earth, and we should be very careful of our life and conduct before those who are *not* of the family of God. I am so glad I am saved! I am so glad I am a member of the Church of the living God, the Church He purchased with His own precious blood, the Church of which He is the Head and against which the gates of hell cannot prevail. The one true Church is the bride of Christ. He is coming soon to catch away His bride, and all believers will be caught up to meet Him in the air (I Thess. 4:13-18).

Dear reader, are YOU a member of the true Church, the Church which was bought with the blood of Jesus? or are you just a member of a local organization, a local denomination? Do you have salvation? or do you have "religion"? If all you have is membership in a local church, then you do not belong to the Church of the living God, neither are you "the habitation of God," for you are lost! If you do not have the witness of the Holy Spirit in your heart to tell you that you are a child of God, I beg you to bow on your knees right now and receive the Lord Jesus as Saviour. Remember—*"As many as RECEIVED Him, to them gave He power to become the sons of God . . ."* (John 1:12).

God Created All Things By Jesus Christ

"Unto me, who am less than the least of all saints, is this grace given, that I should preach among the Gentiles the unsearchable riches of Christ; and to make all men see what is the fellowship of the mystery, which from the beginning of the world hath been hid in God, who CREATED ALL THINGS BY JESUS CHRIST" (Eph. 3:8, 9).

Thus is the heart of the believer assured that God is the Originator and the Organizer of all things. Through the ages men have been searching for an answer to how creation came to be, how man and his surrounding elements came into existence. The answer to that question is plainly given in the Word of God:

"*ALL THINGS were made by HIM,* and without Him was not any thing made that was made" (John 1:3).

"God, who at sundry times and in divers manners spake in time past unto the fathers by the prophets, hath in these last days spoken unto us *by His Son, whom He hath appointed heir of all things, BY WHOM ALSO HE MADE THE WORLDS*" (Heb. 1:1, 2).

The great truth here, beloved, is that "*in the beginning GOD CREATED . . .*" (Gen. 1:1). That is how this earth and everything on it came to be! All things that now exist were created by the eternal Godhead. All things were created *by and for God's Son.* In the beginning *all things* God created were good: "God saw every thing that He had made, and, behold, *it was very good.* And the evening and the morning were the sixth day" (Gen. 1:31).

Yes, even the *devil* was originally good. We know this from the writing of the Prophet Ezekiel. Speaking of the devil before that personage rebelled and attempted to overthrow the Almighty, Ezekiel said, "Thou wast *perfect* in thy ways from the day that thou wast *created,* till iniquity was found in thee" (Ezek. 28:15). So we see that the devil is a created being, but God did not create him a devil! In his original state he was *Lucifer,* the shining one, "son of the morning" (Isa. 14:12). He was "the anointed cherub that covereth" (Ezek. 28:14). We might say he was the high sheriff of the throne of God. But iniquity was found in him and God cast him out of heaven.

Lucifer, the shining one, became the devil, the deceiver, because he decided that he no longer wanted to be subordinate to God. He was ambitious to exalt himself above the throne of God. He would be *greater* than God! As a result of his envy and jealousy he devised an ignominious scheme of rebellion. He deceived some of the angels, leading them to believe that they could help him overthrow God and exalt his throne above the stars of God. But the Creator is greater than the created; and when Satan attempted to carry out his plan, God cast him out of heaven, along with the angels who had chosen to follow him.

In Luke 10:18 Jesus declared, *"I beheld Satan as lightning fall from heaven!"* Many Bible scholars believe that the judgment which rendered the earth "without form and void" struck when God cast Lucifer out of heaven. Be that as it may, we know that at a time which was determined by God after He had created the earth in its original form, judgment did strike—such judgment as the earth has not known since that time—and the earth then became "without form, and void, and darkness was upon the face of the deep" (Gen. 1:2). Certainly a holy, sinless God would not have created the earth as an empty, useless wasteland. Perfection could not create imperfection. In Genesis 1:1 when God created the earth, it was one great and glorious Paradise! *SIN is to blame for the chaos which now reigns throughout the vast creation of God, and sin was born in the heart of Lucifer,* the deceitful and dangerous personality known as "the dragon, that old serpent . . . *the devil . . . Satan"* (Rev. 20:2).

But God brought order out of chaos (Gen. 1:3-31), created man in His own image, planted a beautiful garden in Eden and placed man in that Paradise. Then, His great heart of love and compassion touched by the loneliness of Adam, God caused a deep sleep to fall upon the man. While Adam slept, God removed a rib from his side and from that rib He created woman and gave her to man to be his helpmate (Gen. 2:21-25).

Until that moment in the history of God's re-creation, absolute perfection reigned! All that God had done was good. Earth was a literal Paradise—and would have remained so until this day if sin had not entered. It was because of Adam's sin that God placed a curse upon all creation. The earth today is not as it was when God created it. Man was *created* in the image of God (Gen. 1:26). We do not know to what extent Adam was created in the *visible* image of God nor how much of that likeness he lost in the fall, but we do know he paid a tremendous price for his disobedience to God. Certainly man is not as he was when God created him, nor is woman as she was when she was created in what must have been indescribable beauty and given to Adam for his helpmate!

As Paul expresses it in Romans 8:22, 23, "The *whole creation* groaneth and travaileth in pain together until now—and not only they, but *ourselves* also, which have the firstfruits of the Spirit, *even we ourselves* groan within ourselves, *waiting for the adoption, to wit, the REDEMPTION of our body!*" All creation—including mankind—is longing for that day when the curse will be lifted, when there will be peace on earth and good will among men, and when the earth will be full of the knowledge of the Lord as the waters cover the sea. In that glorious day there will be no more death, neither sorrow or pain. The devil will be in the pit and King Jesus will sit on the throne of David in Jerusalem. That will be the time when *peace* will engulf all of God's creation!

All the Fulness of God

"And to know the love of Christ, which passeth knowledge, that ye might be filled with ALL THE FULNESS OF GOD" (Eph. 3:19).

We can never fully understand the love of Christ —it "passeth knowledge"—but we can know and experience His love in our hearts. All the fulness of God is wrapped up in the love of Christ, but there is no way to explain that love in the terms of man's wisdom:

"For the preaching of the cross is to them that perish foolishness; but unto us which are saved it is the power of God. For it is written, I will destroy the wisdom of the wise, and will bring to nothing the understanding of the prudent. Where is the wise? Where is the scribe? Where is the disputer of this world? Hath not God made foolish the wisdom of this world? For after that in the wisdom of God the world by wisdom knew not God, it pleased God by the foolishness of preaching to save them that believe.

"For the Jews require a sign, and the Greeks seek after wisdom: but we preach Christ crucified, unto the Jews a stumblingblock, and unto the Greeks foolishness; but unto them which are called, both Jews and Greeks, Christ the power of God, and the wisdom of God. Because the foolishness of God is wiser than men; and the weakness of God is stronger than men" (I Cor. 1:18-25).

It is natural to love the lovely. It is easy to love someone who loves us. *But JESUS loved the UNLOVELY!* He even loved and prayed for those who crucified Him—"Father, forgive them; for they know not what they do" (Luke 23:34). Paul tells us, "When we were yet without strength, in due time Christ died *for the ungodly.* . . . God commendeth His love toward us, in that, *while we were yet SINNERS, Christ DIED for us"* (Rom. 5:6, 8). Through Christ's love and grace and through His sacrifice for us, we can enjoy the fulness of the Godhead—not through our own wisdom, but through childlike faith in Him as our personal Saviour and Redeemer.

Above All That We Ask Or Think

"Now unto Him that is able to do exceeding abundantly ABOVE ALL THAT WE ASK OR THINK, according to the power that worketh in us, unto Him be glory in the Church by Christ Jesus throughout all ages, world without end" (Eph. 3:20, 21).

This passage declares God's grace in bestowment. Finite creatures that we are, we cannot *think* in terms of what He is able to do. Men in laboratories spend long hours over microscopes and test tubes, trying to discover the "how" of creation. Archeologists diligently probe ancient ruins for relics of earlier civilizations in their futile search for "the missing link." But the saints of God simply enjoy the fulness of His grace and the abundance of the life which He bestows upon them through their childlike faith in Him as their Redeemer!

The Lord Jesus Christ, our Saviour and our God, is *able to do "exceeding abundantly" ABOVE* anything we can ask or think. Yet in the face of such a declaration there are countless thousands of Christians who are living in the shallow waters of bare necessities when they should be enjoying the deep waters of His abundant supplies! It is every believer's birthright to enjoy the fulness of God's grace, the fulness of His power, and the abundance of heaven's limitless blessings.

It has been said that the Word of God contains 85,000 promises to the believer. I do not doubt that statement. There probably *are* that many promises in the Bible, made to the child of God; but of this I am sure: *Each and every one of those promises carries a condition!* In other words, the promise is contingent upon our doing God's will. He is willing, able, and ready to do *ALL things* for us if we will only hear and obey His Word. For example:

"If ye abide in me, and my words abide in you, ye shall ask what ye will, and it shall be done unto you" (John 15:7). Now let us look at this promise more closely: "If ye *abide* in me" applies only to the believer, for only the believer *could* abide in Jesus. "If . . . *my words* abide in you" means obedience to God's will. *"Ye shall ask WHAT YE WILL, and IT SHALL BE DONE UNTO YOU!"* What a promise! But its fulfillment rests upon our full and complete surrender to Him and our consecration in doing His bidding. After these two conditions have been met we can ask what we will — and it shall be done. Heaven is at the disposal of any Christian who will fully surrender soul, spirit, and body unto the Lord!

Notice God's condition in this promise: "... *No good thing will He withhold from them that walk uprightly*" (Psalm 84:11). God cannot break His Word (Heb. 6:18; Tit. 1:2). Therefore He cannot bless those who do not walk uprightly—and, conversely, *He cannot withhold blessing from those who DO walk uprightly!*

Many Christians say, "I cannot seem to find time to read my Bible, or pray, or witness—and we simply *cannot afford* to tithe." If they really understood the truth of the matter, they would see that they could not afford *not* to find time to read the Bible, pray, witness—and certainly they would see that they could not afford to give less than a tenth of their income to the Lord! Those who take God's time and money and use them for themselves will find that they are losers in the final analysis when God evaluates all things! If you will put Jesus first in everything you do, in everything you are, and in everything you have, *then ALL THAT HE HAS is at your disposal.* He promises, "*Seek ye FIRST the kingdom of God, and His righteousness; and all these things shall be ADDED UNTO YOU*" (Matt. 6:33).

Glory Throughout All Ages

"Unto Him be GLORY in the Church by Christ Jesus THROUGHOUT ALL AGES, world without

end" (Eph. 3:21).

All ages are to witness to the glory and the power of Christ. Even now we who are members of His body sit together in heavenly places in Him (Eph. 2:6); but in the ages to come the Church will be displayed in the Pearly White City, described in Revelation 21:9-27. According to the Word of God, that city will descend from God out of heaven and it will be the capital of God's new creation.

Jesus died for the Church. He purchased it at the tremendous price of His life's blood; and in the eternal ages to come He will have a *perfect* Church without "spot, or wrinkle, or any such thing . . . holy and without blemish" (Eph. 5:27). In the Church He will be glorified *throughout all ages.* Amen! I am so thankful that by means of His saving grace I am a member of that Church. *Are YOU, dear reader?* Check up and make sure that you are truly born again. God's Word warns, "Give diligence to make your calling and election sure" (II Pet. 1:10).

All Lowliness, Meekness, and Longsuffering

"I therefore . . . beseech you that ye walk worthy of the vocation wherewith ye are called, with ALL LOWLINESS AND MEEKNESS, WITH LONG-SUFFERING, forbearing one another in love; endeavouring to keep the unity of the Spirit in the bond of peace" (Eph. 4:1-3).

41

By Grace

"Lowliness" is the mark of real Christian living, and *"meekness"* and *"longsuffering"* are companions of lowliness. The world watches every move the believer makes. Sinners may not read the Bible, but they will read the daily lives of those who profess Christ. One of the outstanding reasons we cannot get sinners to attend church is that so many church people live in just as worldly a fashion as do those who make no profession of Christianity. Such church members are poor advertisements for the cause of Christ and they give the unchurched an opportunity to stand by and say, "I am just as good as they are!"

It is a sad fact that there are many unregenerated church members, and although they may *profess* Christianity, they *conform* to the standards of those who have never been born again. This is one major reason why the local church has lost much of its power to influence the unsaved toward Jesus and salvation. We who name the name of Jesus should be careful how we live, where we go, and what we do. It is a glorious and wonderful privilege to be a child of God; but this relationship with our heavenly Father also imposes upon us a grave responsibility in bearing the name "Christian." When we prove to the world by our daily living that Jesus is truly the Prince of Peace, the all-sufficient One who satisfies every longing of the heart, then *those who do not know Him* will have a *desire* to know Him personally as their

Saviour.

Sinner friend, I would speak this word of warning to you: If you are refusing God's gift of salvation, refusing to come to Jesus, simply because you know some church members who live like the world, the fact that your accusation is true will not cause hell to be any lighter for *you!* You cannot use their hypocrisy as a subterfuge in evading the issue of salvation and your own personal responsibility in choosing where you will spend eternity. It may even be that you live a better life than some of the church members of your acquaintance, but this fact will not lessen the torments of hell for your soul if you refuse to accept the one thing that will keep you *out* of hell—God's gift of His only begotten Son, "that whosoever believeth in Him should not perish, but have everlasting life" (John 3:16).

One God . . . Father of All

"One God and Father of all, who is ABOVE ALL, and THROUGH ALL, and IN you all" (Eph. 4:6).

This does not mean the "Fatherhood of God" in the sense that God is Father of all men. We must remember that Paul wrote his Ephesian letter to the Christians at Ephesus, and *God is the Father of all believers.*

Please notice—*God* and *Father* go together, they are one and the same. Our God is a jealous

God (Ex. 20:3-5). Jesus commanded His disciples, "Call no *man* your father upon the earth: for one is your Father, which is in heaven" (Matt. 23:9). So you see, dearly beloved, we are to refer to no man in a spiritual sense as our father. We have ONE GOD, ONE FATHER, and He is God and Father of all who are *born again.*

Our God is *"above* all." He has no equal. He is not only *mighty, He is ALMIGHTY, omnipotent.* He is *"through all and IN all"*—that is, He lives in the hearts of believers in the Person of the Holy Spirit. Every born again believer has the Holy Spirit dwelling in his heart, and "if any man have not the Spirit of Christ, he is none of His" (Rom. 8:9).

Our God is *ALL-sufficient* for *ALL of His children.* We are COMPLETE in Christ (Col. 2:10). Philippians 4:19 promises, "My God shall supply *ALL your need* according to His riches in glory by Christ Jesus!"

That He Might Fill All Things

"He that descended is the same also that ascended up far above all heavens, that He might FILL ALL THINGS" (Eph. 4:10).

He who was sent to the lowest place now occupies the highest place! Jesus took upon Himself the form of man, and in a body fashioned like unto yours and mine He tasted life from the human standpoint. That is, He "was in all points tempted

44

like as we are, *yet without sin*" (Heb. 4:15). He lived on this earth and moved among men for more than thirty years—sinless, perfect, holy, doing nothing but good. Yet He was condemned by His enemies and sentenced to the most shameful death the mind of man could devise—"even the death of the cross" (Phil. 2:8). Then He descended to the lowest degree—the heart of the earth (Matt. 12:40) in order that we might be exalted to the highest.

He took our place and paid our sin-debt in order that we might spend eternity with Him and share His glory. He bore our sorrow, that we might share His joy. He became sin for us, that we might become partakers of His holiness. He endured the cross, despising its shame, for the joy which was set before Him, "and is set down at the right hand of the throne of God" (Heb. 12:2).

Exalted to the heaven which is far above all heavens, He is now the "one Mediator between God and men, the Man Christ Jesus" (I Tim. 2:5). He lives forevermore, to make intercession for all who will come to Him in childlike faith, believing (Heb. 7:25).

The Unity of All Saints

"And He gave some, apostles; and some, prophets; and some, evangelists; and some, pastors and teachers; for the perfecting of the saints, for the work of the ministry, for the edifying of the body of Christ: till we ALL come IN THE UNITY OF

THE FAITH, and of the knowledge of the Son of God, unto a perfect man, unto the measure of the stature of the fulness of Christ" (Eph. 4:11-13).

The unity of all saints, *"unity of the faith,"* is the ultimate goal to which the Head of the Church is leading. How wonderful it would be if all saved people worked together in unity of the faith—but they do not! God's people do not agree. They are divided—a trick of the devil to hinder the work of the Lord. If all of God's fundamentalist preachers would work together for revival, we would see such revival as this world has not known since Pentecost! Acts 2:1 tells us that the saints at Pentecost were *"all with ONE accord in ONE place."* In other words, *they had UNITY.* They were together, and as they met the requirements of unity, being in complete accord, the Spirit came, the fire fell—and when Peter preached, three thousand souls were saved!

Things are done quite differently today. The Baptists have their revivals, the Methodists have their revivals, other denominations have their revivals or special meetings, and things run according to schedule—or, as they are *expected* to run. The Lord seems not much needed, since there are "committees" to take care of everything. Personalities are introduced as "the outstanding, talented, accomplished" whatever-they-are, and Jesus takes a back seat while men "hold" revivals (which they seldom, if ever, let loose)!

Beloved, where there is *unity in the FAITH* there is *strength!* Where there is *unity in the FAITH* there is *power!* If Christians would *unite in the faith* there would be sweeping revival in this land. But the devil keeps church people so busy fighting *among themselves* that they do not have much time to bother about fighting *him.* He keeps denominational preachers so busy serving and defending the denominations that they have little time to defend the *faith.* O, that we could again have a revival of "the old-time religion" which would, even as in bygone days, *"make us love everybody!"*

Christ—the Head of All Things

"That we henceforth be no more children, tossed to and fro, and carried about with every wind of doctrine, by the sleight of men, and cunning craftiness, whereby they lie in wait to deceive; but speaking the truth in love, may grow up into Him in ALL THINGS, which is the HEAD, even CHRIST" (Eph. 4:14, 15).

In Paul's letter to the Corinthian church he rebuked those believers for remaining "babes in Christ," needing to be fed "with milk, and not with meat" (I Cor. 3:1, 2). There are many spiritual "babies" in the churches of today. They fuss, fight, and pout. Their behavior more fittingly bespeaks that of little children playing in the back yard, than the conduct of mature Christians who have studied to show themselves "approved unto God" (II Tim. 2:15). They have not learned the grace of esteeming others better than themselves (Phil. 2:3). They have not learned the grace of forbearance as Jesus taught it in His Sermon on the Mount. He said, "Whosoever shall smite thee on thy right cheek, *turn to him the other also.* And if any man will sue thee at the law, and take away thy coat, *let him have thy cloke also.* And whosoever shall compel thee to go *a mile,* go with him *twain*" (Matt. 5:39-41). Many believers today need to grow up and put away childish ways.

Paul also rebuked the Corinthians for having allowed divisions to come into the church (I Cor. 1:10-13; 3:3-6). The Corinthian believers had "chosen sides," as it were—the Paulites, the Apollosites, the Cephasites, etc. The spirit of that church has come on down through the years and in all too many instances it is present with us today. Churches have become organized into little "religious cliques." The members of these various groups love those who love them and they do good to those who treat them well. They visit those who visit them in return, and they show kindness to those who have been kind to them. But when they return home after the Sunday morning service they verbally crucify "the other crowd"!

I repeat—many people who are truly born again

are still spiritual babies. This should not be. Feeding on the Word of God they should grow up to be mature Christians. We are to be *childlike* (Matt. 18:3) but not *childish* (I Cor. 13:11), *remembering that ALL SAINTS are members of the SAME BODY and CHRIST is the HEAD of that body.*

Followers of God As Dear Children

"Let all bitterness, and wrath, and anger, and clamour, and evil speaking, be put away from you, with all malice: and be ye kind one to another, tenderhearted, forgiving one another, even as God for Christ's sake hath forgiven you. *Be ye therefore FOLLOWERS OF GOD, AS DEAR CHILDREN;* and walk in love, as Christ also hath loved us, and hath given Himself for us an offering and a sacrifice to God for a sweetsmelling savour.

"But fornication, and all uncleanness, or covetousness, let it not be once named among you, as becometh saints; neither filthiness, nor foolish talking, nor jesting, which are not convenient: but rather giving of thanks. For this ye know, that no whoremonger, nor unclean person, nor covetous man, who is an idolater, hath any inheritance in the kingdom of Christ and of God.

"Let no man deceive you with vain words: for because of these things cometh the wrath of God upon the children of disobedience. Be not ye therefore partakers with them" (Eph. 4:31—5:7).

Sin produces all kinds of uncleanness and all brands of filth. But things are different when we have "so learned Christ" (Eph. 4:20). Sinners walk in the vanity of their minds, and because of the spiritual ignorance and blindness of their hearts they are engulfed in an abyss of spiritual and moral degradation and apathy. Not discerning spiritual matters, they give themselves over to lasciviousness, lustful desires and practices.

But born again people do not so walk. "Therefore if any man be in Christ, *he is a new creature. Old things are passed away; behold, all things are become new*" (II Cor. 5:17). Yes, when we are born again all things become new, but this does not mean that we will not be tempted to sin, nor does it mean that we will not make mistakes. It does mean that whatever is not godly is *ungodly*, whatever is not righteous is *unrighteous*, and the person who *walks after the lusts of the flesh* is not a born again child of God! According to the Scripture just quoted from Paul's letter to the Ephesians (on page 49), people who are guilty of the sins enumerated in those verses are unregenerate sinners, not saints of God. Children of God are to *walk* as children of God. We are to have no fellowship with the unfruitful works of darkness, but rather reprove them; and we are also to warn others concerning the things which bring the wrath of God upon those who are guilty of such works.

All Goodness, Righteousness, and Truth

"For the fruit of the Spirit is in ALL GOOD-NESS and RIGHTEOUSNESS and TRUTH" (Eph. 5:9).

In this verse we see the trinity of the Spirit's fruit. Romans 8:9 tells us that if we have not the Spirit of Christ we are not His, and from our present verse we see that if we profess to be children of God we should prove it before the world by walking in goodness, righteousness, and truth.

Do not misunderstand the meaning here. We do not do good in order to be saved, for good works—no matter how good or how many—will not save us. But *if we ARE saved* we automatically do good because of the goodness of God who abides within our hearts. We will live righteously because of the righteousness of Christ which is imputed to us. Righteousness *within* produces righteousness *without*—i. e., a pure heart produces pure thoughts, pure thoughts produce pure actions. Thus the life of the believer will be pure, setting an example before the unsaved which will create within them a desire to know Christ as their Saviour. We who profess to be saved should take stock of our life and see how our daily living measures up to the trinity of fruits produced by the Spirit. If the *fruit* is not right, there is something wrong with the *tree*. Jesus said, "By their fruits ye shall know them" (Matt. 7:16, 20).

All Things . . . Reproved

"Have no fellowship with the unfruitful works of darkness, but rather REPROVE them. For it is a shame even to speak of those things which are done of them in secret. But ALL THINGS THAT ARE REPROVED are made manifest by the light: for whatsoever doth make manifest is light" (Eph. 5:11-13).

Light reveals wrong and points to the right: "And this is the condemnation, that light is come into the world, and men loved darkness rather than light, because their deeds were evil. For every one that doeth evil hateth the light, neither cometh to the light, lest his deeds should be reproved. But he that doeth truth cometh to the light, that his deeds may be made manifest, that they are wrought in God" (John 3:19-21).

The Word of God is a lamp to our feet, a light to our pathway (Psalm 119:105), and the reason so many church members do not enjoy *reading* the Word of God is because it shows up the ugly places in their lives! It exposes the dirty blotches on their daily living, and since they do not want to *clean up* they will not come to the light. Some church people say, "I see no harm in going where I go, doing what I do, keeping the company I keep." The simple truth is that if they would look into the Word of God, they would be brought to the realization of the error of their ways in many of their habits of life. But they will not come to the light of the Word. Their deeds are evil—but they are not willing to face it. They are not willing for the Word to *reprove* them.

Dear reader, are *you* a Christian with things in your life which sometimes trouble you? Are there some issues before you which you cannot, sincerely and before God, determine the right or wrong involved in them? If so, then read your Bible as a sincere seeker of truth. Keep an open heart and let the Word of God speak to you. Let Him show you the truth, and then follow His leading. The lamp of the Word will show you any evil in your life and the Holy Spirit will lead you into paths of right living for Jesus' sake (Psalm 23:3).

Giving Thanks Always For All Things

"And be not drunk with wine, wherein is excess; but be filled with the Spirit; speaking to yourselves in psalms and hymns and spiritual songs, singing and making melody in your heart to the Lord; GIVING THANKS ALWAYS FOR ALL THINGS unto God and the Father in the name of our Lord Jesus Christ" (Eph. 5:18-20).

Christians are the most unusual people on earth —and rightly so. We are *"a peculiar people"* (I Pet. 2:9), a *heavenly* people (I John 3:1, 2). This is seen in the instructions given in our present verses—that we should *"give thanks always for ALL THINGS."* It is easy enough to be thankful when all goes well—i. e., when loved ones are well, when a pay raise comes along, when business is prospering and the bank account is growing, when men speak well of us and our place in the community seems secure. But *only a CHRISTIAN* can be thankful when things go wrong—when sickness, sorrow, even *death,* darken the way, when disappointment, heartache, and hardships come. The Christian can smile through tears, because *"we know that ALL THINGS work together for good to them that love God, to them who are the called according to His purpose! . . . What shall we then say to these things? If God be FOR us, who CAN be AGAINST us?"* (Rom. 8:28, 31).

Christians live differently because we *are* different. We are children of God, we possess the Holy Spirit, we are partakers of divine nature, and we have within us One who is greater than the one who is in the world. Therefore we do not wait for heaven to show forth the praises of Him who loved us and gave Himself for us. We do not have to wait until Christ calls us home to enjoy heaven's glories—*even now* we sit together in heavenly places in Christ Jesus! (Eph. 2:6).

Paul instructed the Thessalonian believers, *"In EVERY THING give thanks: for this is the will* of God in Christ Jesus concerning you" (I Thess. 5:18). I am not a fatalist. I do not believe the doctrine of "what will be, will be." But I *do* believe that nothing can touch God's child without God's permission! I further believe that a child of God is indispensable on this earth until God has finished with him here, and he has completed the work laid out for him to do.

Having Done All — Stand!

"Finally, my brethren, be strong in the Lord, and in the power of His might. Put on the whole armour of God, that ye may be able to stand against the wiles of the devil. For we wrestle not against flesh and blood, but against principalities, against powers, against the rulers of the darkness of this world, against spiritual wickedness in high places. Wherefore take unto you the whole armour of God, that ye may be able to withstand in the evil day, and HAVING DONE ALL, TO STAND" (Eph. 6:10-13).

In these verses we find valuable information concerning the enemies against whom we fight. Few Christians have ever realized the dangerous and exceeding great power of the foe. Perhaps none of us have ever *fully* comprehended the reality of the deadly warfare in which we are engaged. The enemies against whom we fight are not flesh and blood, but powerful rulers of spiritual wickedness in *high places*. The devil is the god of this world (II Cor. 4:4), he is the prince of the power of the air (Eph. 2:2). He commands a mighty army of demons and wicked spirits, and his strategy is such that mortal man cannot hope to stand against him!

But remember—the Christian is *IN Christ,* and Christ conquered the world, the flesh, the devil, death, hell, and the grave. Therefore *WE are MORE than conquerors through HIM* (Rom. 8:37). We are to put on *His armor*—the *whole armor* of God. If we leave off even one piece of it, the devil will find that exposed spot and attack us through it. But God is bigger and more powerful than the devil, *and if we put on the whole armor of God and determine by the GRACE of God to stand, then we WILL stand!*

The believer who stumbles and falls has only himself to blame. God has provided the armor, and He has provided a way of escape when temptation comes. I Corinthians 10:13 declares, "There hath no temptation taken you but such as is common to man: *but God is faithful, who will not suffer you to be tempted above that ye are able; but will with the temptation also make a way to escape, that ye may be able to bear it.*"

Above All . . . the Shield of Faith

"Stand therefore, having your loins girt about with truth, and having on the breastplate of righteousness; and your feet shod with the preparation

of the Gospel of peace; ABOVE ALL, taking the SHIELD OF FAITH, wherewith ye shall be able to quench all the fiery darts of the wicked. And take the helmet of salvation, and the sword of the Spirit, which is the Word of God" (Eph. 6:14-17).

"Above ALL, taking the shield of faith" indicates that *faith* is the most important part of the armor which God provides for His people. It is true that we are *saved by GRACE,* but saving grace must be *applied* by *faith* (Eph. 2:8). It is *by FAITH* that we overcome the world (I John 5:4). It was *by FAITH* that the outstanding men of the Old Testament accomplished great things for God, as recorded in Hebrews chapter 11:

"By faith ABEL offered unto God a more excellent sacrifice than Cain . . ."* (v. 4).

"By faith ENOCH was translated that he should not see death . . ."* (v. 5).

"By faith NOAH, being warned of God . . . prepared an ark . . ."* (v. 7).

"By faith ABRAHAM, when he was called . . . went out, not knowing whither he went"* (v. 8).

"By faith MOSES . . . refused to be called the son of Pharaoh's daughter, choosing rather to suffer affliction with the people of God, than to enjoy the pleasures of sin for a season"* (vv. 24, 25).

By faith JOSHUA and his people encompassed the city of Jericho, and "by faith the walls of Jericho fell down, after they were compassed about seven days" (v. 30).

"And what shall I more say? for the time would fail me to tell of Gedeon, and of Barak, and of Samson, and of Jephthae; of David also, and Samuel, and of the prophets: who *through faith* subdued kingdoms, wrought righteousness, obtained promises, stopped the mouths of lions, quenched the violence of fire, escaped the edge of the sword, out of weakness were made strong, waxed valiant in fight, turned to flight the armies of the aliens" (vv. 32-34).

It will bless your heart if you will read the entire eleventh chapter in the book of Hebrews, that great chapter which recounts the deeds of many of God's heroes—deeds accomplished *by FAITH in the one and only true God.* So—we must put on "the shield of faith"—but where do we get this shield? Romans 10:17 answers: "Faith cometh *by hearing,* and hearing by the *Word of God."*

The more we live in the pages of our Bible the more faith we will have, and the more efficacious will be our endeavors in overcoming the wicked one. David said, *"Thy Word have I hid in mine heart, that I might not SIN against thee"* (Psalm 119:11).

In Psalm 1:1, 2 we read, "Blessed is the man that walketh not in the counsel of the ungodly, nor standeth in the way of sinners, nor sitteth in the seat of the scornful; but his delight is in the law of the Lord, and in His law (His Word) doth he meditate day and night."

A Bible-loving, Bible-reading, Bible-practicing believer is a victorious believer, for he has "put on the whole armour of God—*and above all, the shield of FAITH,*" with which he is "able to quench *ALL the fiery darts of the wicked.*" The shield of a vital, vibrant, pulsating faith in God is the devil's nemesis, his "Waterloo." He cannot cope with faith. If we depend only on our own ability, power, and discernment, certainly Satan will trip us. We cannot possibly stand against him. But the minute we send Jesus to the door of our hearts, the wicked one is forced to flee in defeat! He can out-argue, out-debate us if we try to defend ourselves in our own strength and wisdom, but he cannot answer *"Thus saith the Lord."* When Jesus encountered the tempter on the Mount of Temptation, He answered every challenge by quoting the Scriptures (Matt. 4:1-11). If *Jesus*, possessing the power *He* possessed, realized His need to use the Word of God in battling the devil, how much *more* do you and I, by comparison, need to be equipped with "the sword of the Spirit," which is the Word!

Praying Always With All Prayer and Supplication

"Praying always with ALL PRAYER and supplication in the Spirit, and watching thereunto with ALL PERSEVERANCE and supplication for ALL

SAINTS" (Eph. 6:18).

The shield of faith is the most important part of our armor, but a shield is no good if it is not correctly used. The only way to have our shields in place, having them ready at all times as protection against "the fiery darts of the wicked," is to *pray without ceasing* (I Thess. 5:17).

Many of us spend long hours in study. We study to preach, we study to teach, we study to help others—and rightly so. But prayer is more important. The Scripture does not record that the disciples ever asked Jesus to teach them how to preach or how to conduct a Bible class—but they did say to Him, *"Lord, teach us to PRAY"* (Luke 11:1).

To Jesus, prayer was more important than teaching and healing: Great multitudes came to hear Him preach and to be healed—*but "He withdrew Himself into the wilderness, and prayed"* (Luke 5:15, 16).

To Jesus, prayer was more important than rest for His body: "In the morning, rising up *a great while before day,* He went out, and departed into a solitary place, and there *prayed"* (Mark 1:35).

To Jesus, prayer was more important than sleep: ". . . He went out into a mountain to pray, *and continued ALL NIGHT in prayer to God"* (Luke 6:12).

To Jesus, prayer was more important than working a miracle. He did not perform a miracle in order to deliver Peter from being sifted of Satan. Instead, *He prayed for him:* "Simon, Simon, behold, Satan hath desired to have you, that he may sift you as wheat: but I have *prayed* for thee, that thy faith fail not . . ." (Luke 22:31, 32).

To Jesus, prayer was more important than machinery or money. When He needed workers He said to His disciples, *"PRAY YE therefore the Lord of the harvest,* that He will send forth labourers into His harvest" (Matt. 9:38).

To Jesus, prayer was more important than preaching. Nowhere in the Scriptures do we read where He taught His disciples to *preach,* but in Matthew 6:5-13 He taught them the prerequisites of prayer, and gave them the well known words of what is commonly referred to as "the Lord's prayer."

To Jesus, the ministry of prayer is more important than all other ministries. This is clearly pointed out in Hebrews 7:25 where we are told that He ever lives to *make intercession* for those who are saved by His grace.

The earthly ministry of Jesus *began* in prayer (Luke 3:21), *continued* in prayer (Luke 6:12; 9:29; 11:1), and *ended* in prayer (Luke 23:34).

Christ's *heavenly* ministry began in prayer— *"I will pray* the Father, and He shall give you another Comforter . . ." (John 14:16), and continues in prayer (Heb. 7:25; I Tim. 2:5). Therefore, even as did His disciples, we need to cry out, *"Lord, teach US to pray!"*

We must also remember that we are not to pray selfishly, praying for self only. We are to pray *"with all perseverance and supplication FOR ALL SAINTS."* All believers are saints of God, and all saints are fighting a common enemy. We are all engaged in the same battle, though not all in the same circumstances nor under the same plan of attack. Satan is clever, he is versatile, he knows the weakness of each and every believer. Thus does he plan his onslaughts. The believer's life should be a life of daily sharing, and that means sharing the burdens of fellow saints. One sure and effective way of sharing is to pray "with all perseverance and supplication *for ALL saints."*

And now I say with Paul, "Peace be to the brethren, *and love with FAITH,* from God the Father and the Lord Jesus Christ. Grace be with all them that love our Lord Jesus Christ in sincerity. Amen!" (Eph. 6:23, 24).

THE BELIEVER'S POSITION IN GRACE

The Believer's Position In Grace

"Paul, called to be an apostle of Jesus Christ through the will of God, and Sosthenes our brother, unto the church of God which is at Corinth, to them that are sanctified in Christ Jesus, called to be saints, with all that in every place call upon the name of Jesus Christ our Lord, both their's and our's: Grace be unto you, and peace, from God our Father, and from the Lord Jesus Christ. I thank my God always on your behalf, for the grace of God which is given you by Jesus Christ; that in every thing ye are enriched by Him, in all utterance, and in all knowledge; even as the testimony of Christ was confirmed in you: so that ye come behind in no gift; waiting for the coming of our Lord Jesus Christ: who shall also confirm you unto the end, that ye may be blameless in the day of our Lord Jesus Christ. God is faithful, by whom ye were called unto the fellowship of His Son Jesus Christ our Lord" (I Cor. 1:1-9).

The believer's position in Christ is *instantaneously* and *fully* entered the moment he receives Jesus by faith. Thus the weakest, most insignificant, most ignorant and fallible born again person has exactly the same relationship in grace as does the most illustrious believer—that is, they both become born again children of God, "saints" of God, the very moment they receive the Lord Jesus Christ as Saviour:

"He that believeth on the Son *hath everlasting life:* and he that believeth not the Son shall not see life; but *the wrath of God* abideth on him" (John 3:36).

"Beloved, *NOW are we the sons of God,* and it doth not yet appear what we shall be: but we know that, when He shall appear, we shall be like Him; for we shall see Him as He is" (I John 3:2).

"He that hath the Son *hath life;* and he that hath not the Son of God *hath not life"* (I John 5:12).

In this message we will discuss the sphere of the saints. Born again believers, *"called to be saints,"* are IN CHRIST, and in Christ it is the spiritual birthright of every born again believer to enjoy *full joy* and *abundant life.* However, it is impossible for a believer to claim his spiritual birthright without knowing the position, possession, and prospect of *the believer IN Christ.* All that we are, all that we have, all that we will ever be or ever have is in Christ—*"for OF Him, and THROUGH Him, and TO Him, are all things:* to whom be glory for ever. Amen!" (Rom. 11:36).

David did not have the glorious New Testament Scriptures, but he knew the Lord and enjoyed spiritual fellowship with God. He testified:

"Truly my soul waiteth upon God. From Him

cometh my salvation. He only is my rock and my salvation. He is my defence; I shall not be greatly moved. . . . My soul, wait thou only upon God; for my expectation is from Him. He only is my rock and my salvation. He is my defence; I shall not be moved. In God is my salvation and my glory. *The rock of my strength, and my refuge, is IN GOD"* (Psalm 62:1-7 in part).

Jehovah God was the sphere in which David moved, the element in which he delighted, the atmosphere in which he breathed, the circle that separated him from all else. His environment was above the world—he lived and moved in heavenly places. The sphere of the believer today is described as being *"IN Christ Jesus."*

Yes, it is altogether possible, even in these dark days in which we live, for the Christian to live in heavenly places beyond the seductions of the flesh, beyond the realm of discouragement and circumstance, beyond the folly of pride and beyond the confusion of this world. With this in mind, I want us to study seven references made by the Apostle Paul—statements in which the expression "IN CHRIST JESUS" occurs. These references are found in Paul's second letter to Timothy, his son in the faith.

I
"Life . . . In Christ Jesus"

"Paul, an apostle of Jesus Christ by the will of

God, according to *the promise of life which is IN CHRIST JESUS"* (II Tim. 1:1).

The "life" Paul speaks of here has reference to greater life than physical, mental, moral, or social life. He is speaking of *"THE Life,"* as Jesus said to Thomas, "I am the Way, the Truth, *and THE LIFE . . ."* (John 14:6). God is the Giver of life: "The wages of sin is death; but *the GIFT of God is ETERNAL LIFE through Jesus Christ our Lord"* (Rom. 6:23). Therefore God, the Author of life, is the only One who can give life as spoken of in our present passage from Paul's letter to Timothy.

In John 1:4 we read, *"In Him* (Christ) *was LIFE;* and *the LIFE* was the light of men."

In John 17:1-3 Jesus prayed, "Father, the hour is come; glorify thy Son, that thy Son also may glorify thee: as thou hast given Him power over all flesh, *that He should GIVE ETERNAL LIFE* to as many as thou hast given Him. And *this is LIFE ETERNAL, that they might know thee the only true God, and Jesus Christ,* whom thou hast sent."

God the Father so loved the world that He gave His only Son to take the sinner's place, pay sin's debt, and make it possible for hell-deserving sinners to have eternal life and be delivered from the damnation of eternal destruction. God the Father is the Giver of eternal life—and the life He gives is *Christ*. Therefore the only way to know God is *THROUGH Christ*.

God's love-gift to sinners was His only begotten Son. The *Son's* love-gift to sinners was His life. Just before Jesus went to Calvary He declared, "Therefore doth my Father love me, because I lay down my life, that I might take it again. No man taketh it from me, but I lay it down of myself. I have power to lay it down, and I have power to take it again. This commandment have I received of my Father" (John 10:17, 18). Jesus laid His life down to pay sin's debt, that believers, *in Him,* might live eternally.

The INSTRUMENT *of life is the Word of God:*

". . . our Saviour Jesus Christ . . . hath abolished death, and hath brought life and immortality to light through *the Gospel*" (II Tim. 1:10).

In I Corinthians 15:1-4, the Apostle Paul defines the Gospel as *the death, burial, and resurrection of Jesus "according to the Scriptures."*

Peter tells us that we are born again "not of *corruptible* seed, but of *incorruptible, by the WORD OF GOD,* which liveth and abideth for ever" (I Pet. 1:23). It is a divine impossibility to receive eternal life apart from the Word of God. In fact, one must hear the Word of God in order to know that *there is* life eternal for the believer. The sinner is saved through calling on the name of the Lord—but he cannot call in faith believing until he first believes the Gospel message. He cannot believe the Gospel message until he hears it, and he cannot hear the Gospel message until someone declares it. We find a very clear outline of this truth in Romans 10:13-17:

"For whosoever shall call upon the name of the Lord shall be saved. How then shall they call on Him in whom they have not believed? And how shall they believe in Him of whom they have not heard? And how shall they hear without a preacher? And how shall they preach, except they be sent? As it is written, How beautiful are the feet of them that preach the Gospel of peace, and bring glad tidings of good things! . . . So then *faith* cometh by *hearing,* and *hearing* by THE WORD OF GOD."

Jesus did not come into the world that there might be a Gospel to preach. *He IS the Gospel, the WORD Incarnate:*

"In the beginning was the Word, and the Word was with God, and the Word was God. The same was in the beginning with God. . . . And the Word was made flesh, and dwelt among us, (and we beheld His glory, the glory as of the only begotten of the Father,) full of grace and truth. . . . No man hath seen God at any time. The only begotten Son, which is in the bosom of the Father, He hath declared Him" (John 1:1, 2, 14, 18).

Yes, Jesus was the Word in flesh. He came into the world to make known God's love, mercy, and grace. He said, "Verily, verily, I say unto you, *He that heareth my WORD,* and believeth on Him that sent me, hath *everlasting LIFE*, and shall not come into condemnation; but is passed from death unto life" (John 5:24).

In His message on the bread of life, Jesus declared: "I am the living bread which came down from heaven. If any man eat of this bread, he shall live for ever. And the bread that I will give is my flesh, which I will give for the life of the world. . . . Verily, verily, I say unto you, Except ye eat the flesh of the Son of man, and drink His blood, *ye have no LIFE in you*" (John 6:51, 53).

Then in verse 63 of that same chapter He explained the meaning of those words: "It is the Spirit that quickeneth; the flesh profiteth nothing. *The WORDS that I speak unto you, they are spirit, and they are LIFE.*" Many of His followers then turned back and refused to walk with Him, and turning to the twelve He asked of them, *"Will ye also go away?"* Peter replied, "Lord, to whom shall we go? *Thou hast the WORDS of eternal LIFE!*" (John 6:66-68). So we see that Peter understood what Jesus meant when He said, "Except ye eat my flesh and drink my blood, ye have no life in you."

The only way for a sinner to be saved, made alive in Christ, is for him to *hear* and *appropriate* the Word of God. Faith comes by hearing, faith brings salvation, and salvation is God's gift to lost, hell-deserving souls.

The POWER of life is the Holy Spirit:

"He came unto His own, and His own received Him not. *But as MANY AS RECEIVED HIM, to them gave He POWER to become the sons of God,* even to them that believe on His name: which were born—not of blood, nor of the will of the flesh, nor of the will of man, but of GOD" (John 1:11-13).

We are born into God's family through the power of God—"not by might, nor by power, but *by MY SPIRIT,* saith the Lord of hosts" (Zech. 4:6). Jesus explained to Nicodemus, "Except a man be born of water *and of the SPIRIT,* he cannot enter into the kingdom of God" (John 3:5). When the unbeliever *hears* and *believes* the Word, the power of the Holy Spirit "borns" that unbeliever into God's family by and through the Word of God.

In dealing with redemption, it is impossible to separate Father, Son, Holy Spirit, and the Word, for they all have a definite part in salvation. Jesus said, "No man can come to me, except the Father which hath sent me draw him . . ." (John 6:44), and in John 16:7-11 He explains *how* the Father draws men to Him:

"Nevertheless I tell you the truth: It is expedient for you that I go away: for if I go not away, the Comforter will not come unto you; but if I depart, I will send Him unto you. And when He is come, He will reprove the world of sin, and of righteousness, and of judgment. Of sin, because they believe not on me. Of righteousness, because I go to my Father, and ye see me no more. Of judgment, because the prince of this world is judged."

The Holy Spirit convicts men of *sin*, of *righteousness*, and of *judgment*—and He always uses the Word to bring conviction to an unbelieving heart. "For the Word of God is *quick*, and *powerful*, and *sharper than any twoedged sword*, piercing even to the dividing asunder of soul and spirit, and of the joints and marrow, and is a discerner of the thoughts and intents of the heart" (Heb. 4:12).

Apart from hearing the Word, there can be no conviction of sin. Paul said, ". . . I had not known lust, except the law had said, *Thou shalt not covet*" (Rom. 7:7b), and in Romans 3:20 we read: "Therefore by the deeds of the law there shall no flesh be justified in His sight: for *by the law is the knowledge of SIN!*"

When one believes on the Lord Jesus Christ and becomes the recipient of eternal life, that individual is born into the family of God, he becomes a member of the body of Christ—and this miracle occurs through the power of the Holy Spirit:

"For as the body is one, and hath many members, and all the members of that one body, being many, are one body: so also is Christ. *For by ONE SPIRIT are we all baptized into one body,* whether we be Jews or Gentiles, whether we be bond or free; and have been all made to drink into one Spirit" (I Cor. 12:12, 13).

The Holy Spirit convicts the sinner of sin, of righteousness, and of judgment. He draws the unbeliever to Christ, "borns" him into the family of God through the miracle of the new birth by the incorruptible seed (the living Word), unites the believer to the body of Christ and then takes up His abode in the inner man. Thus the Holy Spirit *dwells* in the heart of the believer and "if any man *have NOT* the Spirit of Christ, he is none of His" (Rom. 8:9).

The Holy Spirit *leads* the child of God into paths of righteousness, "for as many as are *led* by the Spirit of God, they are *the sons of God*" (Rom. 8:14).

The Holy Spirit gives *unshakeable assurance* to the heart of the believer, assurance that he is a born again child of God: "The Spirit Himself beareth witness with our spirit, that we are the children of God" (Rom. 8:16).

The Holy Spirit *seals* the believer "unto the day of redemption"—that is, the redemption of the body (Eph. 4:30).

The Holy Spirit *fills* all who will allow such filling (Eph. 5:18), but before we can be filled with the Spirit we must allow Him to *empty us* of all that would hinder Him. We must allow Him to search our hearts and lives, and remove any and all things that are not Christ-like. It is when we yield ourselves unreservedly to God—soul, spirit, and body—that the Holy Spirit fills us and lets us know the joy of our spiritual birthright, "joy unspeakable and full of glory" (I Pet. 1:8).

Throughout the earthly sojourn of a believer—from the moment he is saved until he enters the Pearly White City and the eternal ages begin—the Holy Spirit never ceases to minister to the believer and his interests. Romans 8:11 tells us that "the Spirit of Him that raised up *Jesus* from the dead" will also quicken *our* mortal bodies.

The CONSUMMATION of life is glory:

"If ye then be risen with Christ, seek those things which are above, where Christ sitteth on the right hand of God. Set your affection on things above, not on things on the earth. For ye are dead, and your life is hid with Christ in God. *When Christ, who is our LIFE, shall appear, then shall ye also appear with Him IN GLORY*" (Col. 3:1-4).

Since we as believers are dead to sin and alive unto God, we should seek those things which are *above*. Since we are dead to the world, hid with Christ in God, we should *set our affection* on "things above." If we serve God wholeheartedly in this life, we will suffer heartaches, persecutions, and tribulations; but we can say with Paul "that the sufferings of this present time are not worthy to be compared with the GLORY which shall be revealed in us" (Rom. 8:18).

Romans 8:28-30 assures us "that all things work together for good *to them that love God,* to them who are the called according to *His purpose.* For whom He did *foreknow,* He also did *predestinate* to be conformed to the image of His Son, that He might be the firstborn among many brethren. Moreover whom He did predestinate, them He also *called:* and whom He called, them He also *justified:* and whom He justified, *them He also GLORIFIED."*

All things that happen to a born again believer, from the time he believes until he is received into Paradise, work together for his good and God's glory, molding and making him what he ought to be. According to God's Word, every believer is destined to be conformed to the image of God's Son, and every justified soul will eventually be glorified. God allows us to suffer in order that we may be molded and made into a vessel meet for His use, a vessel that will bring glory to His name.

In his letter to the church at Ephesus, Paul gives a word-picture of unbelievers—dead in trespasses and sins, walking "according to the course of this world, according to the prince of the power of the air . . . children of disobedience," having conversation in the lusts of the flesh and fulfilling the *desires* of the flesh—*"by nature* the children

of wrath." And then he thunders out, *"BUT GOD,*
who is rich in mercy, for His great love wherewith
He loved us, even when we were dead in sins,
hath quickened us together with Christ, (by grace
ye a.e saved;) and hath raised us up together, and
made us sit together in heavenly places in Christ
Jesus: *That in the ages to come He might shew
the exceeding riches of His grace in His kindness
toward us through Christ Jesus"* (Eph. 2:1-7).

The future home of the New Testament Church
(the bride of Christ) will be the Pearly White City
described in Revelation chapter 21. I believe the
Scripture indicates that this glorious city will be
suspended between the third heaven (God's house)
and the new earth, and throughout all eternity
God will display the exceeding riches of His grace
toward us as the bride of Christ occupies the home
now being prepared for the Church.

II
"Called . . . In Christ Jesus"

"Who hath saved us, and *CALLED us* with
an holy calling, not according to our works, but
according to His own purpose and grace, which
was given us *in Christ Jesus* before the world
began" (II Tim. 1:9).

God "hath SAVED us." We are not saved
progressively. We are saved instantaneously, saved
with a perfect salvation provided by a perfect God.
"Salvation belongeth unto the Lord . . ." (Psalm

3:8). "Salvation is of the Lord" (Jonah 2:9). "Not by works of righteousness which we have done, but according to His mercy He saved us, by the washing of regeneration, and renewing of the Holy Ghost" (Tit. 3:5).

"*. . . and called us with an HOLY calling.*" The God who calls us is a holy God, and that to which the believer is called is also holy. Therefore the calling of God is holy—and since it comes wholly from God it claims the called one wholly (completely). Bible holiness, Bible sanctification, Bible election and predestination, the sovereignty of God—these are great truths set forth in the Word. Yet many true believers have cheated themselves because of the abuse of these truths by some "religions" and denominations. There is no reason for any born again believer to fear "holiness." We study the Holy Bible, we read about our holy God who saves us with His holy salvation. But there is a great need for Christians to *understand* the Bible doctrine of holiness.

Our holiness is *in Christ.* We are holy because He abides in us in the Person of the Holy Spirit. God does not save us "according to our works, but *according to His own purpose and grace, which was given to us IN CHRIST JESUS.*" The Word of God clearly teaches that *without holiness* no man shall see God (Heb. 12:14). Therefore we need to face *Bible truth* concerning holiness.

Spiritual ignorance robs believers of their spiritual birthright. Paul prayed earnestly that the believers in the churches he established would not be ignorant concerning great Bible truths. To the Colossian believers he wrote, "For this cause we also . . . do not cease to pray for you, and to desire that ye might be filled with the knowledge of His will in all wisdom and spiritual understanding; that ye might walk worthy of the Lord unto all pleasing, being fruitful in every good work, and increasing in the knowledge of God; strengthened with all might, according to His glorious power, unto all patience and longsuffering with joyfulness; giving thanks unto the Father, which hath made us meet to be partakers of the inheritance of the saints in light: who hath delivered us from the power of darkness, and hath translated us into the kingdom of His dear Son: in whom we have redemption through His blood, even the forgiveness of sins" (Col. 1:9-14).

Here we see that Paul was concerned that his converts increase in knowledge and understanding, and that they not forget to give thanks to God for their translation from the kingdom of darkness (the kingdom of Satan) into the kingdom of light (the kingdom of God's dear Son). The sphere into which the Christian is called is the kingdom of light, the kingdom of holiness, of shekinah glory. We sit together in heavenly places in Christ Jesus.

Peter expresses the same truth in these words: "Ye are a chosen generation, a royal priesthood, an holy nation, a peculiar people; that ye should shew forth the praises of Him who hath called you out of darkness into His marvellous light" (I Pet. 2:9).

John the Beloved further explains, "This then is the message which we have heard of Him, and declare unto you, that *GOD IS LIGHT, and in Him is no darkness at all.* If we say that we have fellowship with Him, and walk in darkness, we lie, and do not the truth: *but if we walk in the light, as HE is in the light, we have fellowship one with another, and the blood of Jesus Christ His Son cleanseth us from all sin"* (I John 1:5-7).

Verses 8-10 of this same chapter explain what it means to "walk in the light":

"If we say that we have no sin, we deceive ourselves, and the truth is not in us. If we *confess* our sins, He is faithful and just to *forgive* us our sins, and to cleanse us from all unrighteousness. If we say that we have not sinned, we make Him a liar, *and His Word is not in us."*

Christ in the heart (in the Person of the Holy Spirit) reminds us of sin in our nature and convicts us of sins in our life, and the blood of God's Son makes provision for both. The blood of Jesus takes away *the sin of unbelief* that would damn the soul, and it washes away *sins* that would rob the Christian of fellowship with God and reward at the end of this life. S-I-N (singular) damns. S-I-N-S (plural) interrupt fellowship and rob the believer of reward. But when the sinner *believes on Jesus,*

God saves that soul for Christ's sake; and when God's "little children" confess their sins, God forgives—and fellowship is restored. Thus we understand that "walking in the light" means *unbroken fellowship with God.*

"WHEREFORE—gird up the loins of your mind, be sober, and hope to the end for the grace that is to be brought unto you at the revelation of Jesus Christ; *as obedient children, not fashioning yourselves according to the former lusts in your IGNORANCE: but as He which hath called you is HOLY, so be ye holy in all manner of conversation; because it is written, Be YE holy, for I AM HOLY"* (I Pet. 1:13-16).

The thought of holiness frightens some believers, but such fear is due to spiritual ignorance. In other words, *our "holiness"* is Christ abiding in our hearts. Thus we possess *His holiness,* His *righteousness,* His *wisdom.* Christ "is made unto us wisdom, and righteousness, and sanctification, and redemption: that, according as it is written, He that glorieth, let him glory in the Lord" (I Cor. 1:30, 31).

We must remember that "that which is born of the flesh is flesh, and *that which is born of the Spirit is spirit"* (John 3:6). Then in I John 3:5-9 we read these assuring words:

"Ye know that He (Christ) was manifested to take away our sins; and *IN HIM is no sin.* Whosoever abideth in Him sinneth not. Whosoever

81

sinneth hath not seen Him, neither known Him.

"Little children, let no man deceive you: he that doeth righteousness is righteous, even as He is righteous. He that committeth sin is of the devil; for the devil sinneth from the beginning. For this purpose the Son of God was manifested, that He might destroy the works of the devil. *Whosoever is BORN OF GOD doth not commit sin; for His seed remaineth in him: and he cannot sin, BECAUSE he is born of God!"*

If we will study these verses carefully we will understand that Jesus "was manifested (that is, came into the world) to take away our sins." In *Him* is no sin—He is the sinless One, He knew no sin. The believer is *IN Christ*, the Righteous One. Therefore God sees the believer as He sees Christ— sinless and holy. He sees us "accepted in the Beloved" (Eph. 1:6).

Verse 9 in this passage from I John declares, *"Whosoever is born of God* (not the flesh, but the inner man) *doth not commit sin."* Why? *BECAUSE God's seed* (the seed is the Word, the Word is Christ, and Christ is God) *"remaineth in him and he CANNOT sin."*

Believers are called to walk in the footsteps of Jesus (I Pet. 2:21), and the only possible way we can follow in His steps is to be led by Him. David knew and expressed this truth when he penned the Twenty-Third Psalm. He declared, *"The LORD is my Shepherd. . . . He leadeth me in the paths of righteousness* (the paths of right living) *for His name's sake"* (Psalm 23:1, 3).

"Ye are all *the children of LIGHT,* and the *children of the DAY.* We are not of the night, nor of darkness" (I Thess. 5:5). Believers are God's lights in a dark world. Jesus said, "As long as I am *IN the world,* I am the *LIGHT of the world"* (John 9:5). But Jesus is now in heaven where He sits at the Father's right hand, and we are His representatives on earth—we are His lights. We may not all be beacons on a hill, but we *can* all be "lower lights." We can let our light shine as we are commanded to do, *that men may see our good works, and glorify our Father which is in heaven* (Matt. 5:16). As lights in a dark world believers are called to exhibit the graces of humility, meekness, longsuffering and unity among brethren. We are called to live peaceably among ourselves because we know *the Prince of Peace* who called us with a holy calling.

I love the opening verses of II Peter, chapter 1, where we read:

"Simon Peter, a servant and an apostle of Jesus Christ, to them that have obtained like precious faith with us through the righteousness of God and our Saviour Jesus Christ: Grace and peace be multiplied unto you through the knowledge of God, and of Jesus our Lord, according as His divine power hath given unto us all things that pertain unto life and godliness, through the knowledge of *Him that hath called us to GLORY AND VIR-TUE:*

"Whereby are given unto us exceeding great and precious promises: that by these ye might be *partakers of the divine nature,* having escaped the corruption that is in the world through lust. And beside this, giving all diligence, add to your faith virtue; and to virtue knowledge; and to knowledge temperance; and to temperance patience; and to patience godliness; and to godliness brotherly kindness; and to brotherly kindness charity. *For if these things be in you, and abound, they make you that ye shall neither be barren nor unfruitful in the knowledge of our Lord Jesus Christ"* (II Pet. 1:1-8).

The believer is also called to enjoy many spiritual blessings:

Life:—

In I Timothy 6:12 Paul instructed young Timothy, "Fight the good fight of faith, lay hold on *eternal LIFE, whereunto thou art also called,* and hast professed a good profession before many witnesses." There was no doubt in Paul's mind that eternal life is a *present possession.*

Liberty:—

To the Galatians Paul wrote, "For, brethren, ye have been *called unto LIBERTY;* only use not liberty for an occasion to the flesh, but by love serve one another" (Gal. 5:13). In verse 1 of the same chapter in Galatians, Paul warned them to "stand fast . . . in the liberty wherewith Christ hath made us free, and be not entangled again with the yoke of bondage." Christ had made them free from the law—and "if the Son therefore shall make you free, ye shall be free indeed" (John 8:36). Made free in Christ, the Galatians were to recognize their liberty, and they were not to attempt to mix law and grace. Such liberty, however, is not to be used to satisfy the desires of the flesh, but rather to serve one another in love.

Peace:—

"But if the unbelieving depart, let him depart. A brother or a sister is not under bondage in such cases. But *God hath called us to PEACE*" (I Cor. 7:15). This seventh chapter of I Corinthians is given to instructing believers concerning marriage and divorce. Paul tells them if the unbelieving mate departs from the believing wife or husband, the believer is not in bondage under such conditions because *"God hath called us to peace,"* and we must *live* in peace. Therefore if the unbelieving mate desires to leave the Christian, the believing one is not to force the unbeliever to remain. It is far better for husband and wife to separate and live apart than to live in continual discord, quarreling and bickering in the home. The same is true in other walks of life—on the job, in the church, wherever we may be. Called to peace, we should, insofar as is possible, "live peaceably with all men" (Rom. 12:18).

By Grace

Fellowship: —

The *apex* of the believer's calling is *personal fellowship with Christ:* "God is faithful, by whom ye were called unto *the fellowship of His Son Jesus Christ our Lord*" (I Cor. 1:9). How glorious to be able to walk and talk with Christ! but even more glorious is the assurance that He abides in our heart. He has promised, "I will never leave thee, nor forsake thee" (Heb. 13:5). He said, "Lo, I am with you alway, even unto the end of the world" (Matt. 28:20).

In John 14:16-20 Jesus promised the disciples, "I will pray the Father, and He shall give you another Comforter, that He may *abide with you for ever*—even the Spirit of truth, whom the world cannot receive, because it seeth Him not, neither knoweth Him: *but ye know Him; for He dwelleth with you, and shall be IN YOU*. I will not leave you comfortless: I will come to you. Yet a little while, and the world seeth me no more; but ye see me: because I live, ye shall live also. At that day ye shall know that *I am in my Father, and ye in me, and I in you.*"

These comforting words followed Christ's promise to His disciples that although He was going away, He would return and take them unto Himself, that they might live with Him in the place He was going to prepare for them. But until His return, the Comforter, the Holy Spirit, would be with them and would *dwell WITHIN them.* So we have the Holy Spirit within our hearts. He walks with us, talks with us, guides us, assures us, and seals us. And one glorious day He will raise our mortal bodies and we will have bodies like the glorious resurrection body of Jesus.

I repeat—the apex of the calling of the believer is personal fellowship with Christ.

III
"Hold Fast . . . In Christ Jesus"

"Hold fast the form of sound words, which thou hast heard of me, in faith and love which is *in Christ Jesus"* (II Tim. 1:13).

What is the believer to "hold fast"? He is to hold fast *"the form of sound words."* The *manner* in which the form of sound words is to be held is *"IN Christ Jesus."*

The meaning of "hold fast" is *"to have and to hold."* Therefore the form of sound words is *a continuous possession.* Paul was jealous with godly jealousy for the pure Gospel of the grace of God, without mixture. He often warned concerning false teachers and those who deviated from pure Gospel and turned to error. We can sense his anxiety and earnestness of soul as he cried out, *"O Timothy! Keep that which is committed to thy trust,* avoiding profane and vain babblings, and oppositions of science falsely so called, *which some professing have erred concerning the faith . . ."* (I Tim. 6:20, 21). It is entirely possible that

Paul had such people in mind when he penned the words of our text, warning young Timothy to "hold fast the form of sound words."

In II Timothy 2:15-18 Paul urges Timothy to study to shew himself "approved unto God, a workman that needeth not to be ashamed, rightly dividing the Word of truth," and then he spoke of "Hymenaeus and Philetus, *who concerning the truth have erred,* saying that the resurrection is past already; and *overthrow the faith of some.*"

Now there is only one way for the believer to "hold fast," and that is *to be HELD*—held by the power of Almighty God. Many times believers (in ignorance) ask fellow believers to pray for them, that they will "hold out faithfully to the end." Actually, what we need to pray for is sufficient consecration to allow God to get a firm grip on us, for we are not strong enough to *"hold OUT"* or *"hold ON."* It is only when we are held by God's mighty hand that we can "hold fast," and the only way for us to be held by the hand of God is through faith "in Christ Jesus."

One of my favorite passages in all of the Word of God is Romans chapter 8. This chapter *begins* "IN CHRIST" and *ends* "IN CHRIST." The first verse of Romans 8 reads, "There is therefore now *no condemnation to them which are IN CHRIST JESUS,* who walk not after the flesh, but after the Spirit," and the last verse in the chapter reads, ". . . nor height, nor depth, nor any other creature, shall be able to separate us from the love of God *which is IN CHRIST JESUS our Lord.*"

The meaning of Romans 8:1 is that those who are *IN Christ Jesus* do not walk after the flesh, but after the Spirit. They walk after the Spirit because they are *led* by the Spirit. He dwells in the heart of every born again believer. The verse does not say, "There is therefore now no condemnation to them who are in Christ Jesus *IF they walk not after the flesh.*" The born again Christian will not walk after the flesh because he is led of the *Spirit,* and "if any man *have NOT* the Spirit of Christ, he is none of His" (Rom. 8:9).

The Christian life *begins* in Christ, *continues* in Christ, and *climaxes* in Christ insofar as our earthly life is concerned. Therefore it is *only in Christ Jesus* that we are able to "*hold fast* the form of sound words."

IV
"Grace . . . In Christ Jesus"

"Thou therefore, my son, be strong in the *grace* that is *IN CHRIST JESUS*" (II Tim. 2:1).

All spiritual blessings are the result of grace, and grace is God's unmerited, unearned, undeserved favor toward man. There is nothing man can do, give, live, or be in order to merit grace. Grace is bestowed upon believers because of our faith in the finished work of Christ. Salvation is *all of grace,* without mixture. "And if by grace, then it is no more of works: otherwise grace is no more grace. But if it be of works, then is it no more grace: otherwise work is no more work" (Rom. 11:6).

"In Christ Jesus" believers are *established in grace*. In Hebrews 13:1-9 the Apostle Paul admonishes:

"Let brotherly love continue. Be not forgetful to entertain strangers: for thereby some have entertained angels unawares. Remember them that are in bonds, as bound with them; and them which suffer adversity, as being yourselves also in the body. . . . Let your conversation be without covetousness; and be content with such things as ye have: for He hath said, I will never leave thee, nor forsake thee. So that we may boldly say, The Lord is my helper, and I will not fear what man shall do unto me.

"Remember them which have the rule over you, who have spoken unto you the Word of God: whose faith follow, considering the end of their conversation. Jesus Christ the same yesterday, and to day, and for ever. *Be not carried about with divers and strange doctrines. For it is a good thing that the heart be ESTABLISHED WITH GRACE;* not with meats, which have not profited them that have been occupied therein."

In other words, Paul wanted these believers to understand that they should be established with *grace,* not with the rituals of the law such as abstaining from meats or practicing rituals which were observed under the Mosaic system. *Grace is CHRIST*, and Christ in the heart of the believer is all-sufficiency. There is nothing that can be added. God looks upon the heart, and when we serve Him with whole-hearted dedication we will eat right, drink right, and live right. Thus the Christian is *established with grace*—not with meats, drinks, observance of days, or rituals.

The supply of grace is unlimited:—

Christ is grace, Christ is in the believer and the believer is in Christ. Therefore—the supply of grace to the believer is unlimited. *"Where sin abounded, GRACE did much more abound"* (Rom. 5:20b). The sin-question has been settled—once and forever—through the one sacrifice of the Lord Jesus Christ who entered into the holiest with His own blood and satisfied God by the offer of Himself. Therefore, "As sin hath reigned unto death, even so might grace reign through righteousness unto eternal life by Jesus Christ our Lord" (Rom. 5:21).

The grace of God is all-sufficient:—

The Apostle Paul knew this from personal experience, and testified to that fact. In II Corinthians 12:7-9 he said:

"Lest I should be exalted above measure . . . there was given to me a thorn in the flesh, the messenger of Satan to buffet me, lest I should be exalted above measure. For this thing I besought the Lord thrice, that it might depart from me. And He said unto me, *MY GRACE is sufficient for thee: for my strength is made perfect in weakness.* Most gladly therefore will I rather glory in my infirmities, that the power of Christ may rest upon me."

There has been much discussion and speculation as to what Paul's "thorn in the flesh" might have been. The Word of God does not reveal that detail, but it does record God's specific promise to Paul concerning the all-sufficiency of His grace. We know that Paul found this promise to be true, because just before he sealed his testimony with his life's blood—not as pastor of an outstanding church in a great city, but in a Roman jail—he wrote to Timothy, his son in the ministry:

"I am now ready to be offered, and the time of my departure is at hand. I have fought a good fight, I have finished my course, I have kept the faith. Henceforth there is laid up for me a crown of righteousness, which the Lord, the righteous Judge, shall give me at that day: and not to me only, but unto all them also that love His appearing" (II Tim. 4:6-8).

Paul found that the grace of God was sufficient under any and all circumstances, and you and I will find it so when we put God to the test! Regardless of the need of the individual believer,

God's grace is sufficient—in health or in sickness, in plenty or in want, in happiness or in sorrow, in life or in death—when the moment arrives that we need grace, God gives *an abundance of grace,* grace sufficient for any need.

Furthermore, the Apostle Paul testified, "I am the least of the apostles, that am not meet to be called an apostle, because I persecuted the Church of God. BUT—*by THE GRACE OF GOD I am what I am:*   and His grace which was bestowed upon me was not in vain; but I laboured more abundantly than they all: *yet not I, but THE GRACE OF GOD which was with me"* (I Cor. 15:9, 10).

Believers are admonished to GROW in grace:—

We do not *grow INTO* grace, we are recipients of the grace of God through faith in the finished work of Jesus. But grace stimulates us and puts within us a desire to grow. We are instructed, "Grow in grace, and in the knowledge of our Lord and Saviour Jesus Christ. . ." (II Pet. 3:18).

By the grace of God, the believer is brought into the highest conceivable position spiritually:

"Blessed be the God and Father of our Lord Jesus Christ, who hath blessed us with all spiritual blessings in heavenly places in Christ: according as He hath chosen us in Him before the foundation of the world, that we should be holy and without blame before Him in love: having predestinated us unto the adoption of children by Jesus Christ to Himself, according to the good pleasure of His will, to the praise of *the glory of His GRACE,* wherein He hath made us accepted in the Beloved, in whom we have redemption through His blood, the forgiveness of sins, *according to the riches of His GRACE"* (Eph. 1:3-7).

However, grace does not cease to work for us when we are saved and made accepted in the Beloved. God works ceaselessly through grace—and to the believer He imparts *MANY graces—the fruit of the Spirit:*

"The fruit of the Spirit is *love, joy, peace, long-suffering, gentleness, goodness, faith, meekness, temperance:* against such there is no law" (Gal. 5:22, 23).

The grace of God teaches and instructs us:—

"For *the grace of God that bringeth salvation* hath appeared to all men, *TEACHING US that, denying ungodliness and worldly lusts, we should live soberly, righteously, and godly, in this present world,* looking for that blessed hope, and the glorious appearing of the great God and our Saviour Jesus Christ" (Tit. 2:11-13).

Many unbelievers say, "I believe I could be saved, but I could never *overcome evil!"* Certainly we cannot overcome evil in our own strength any more than we can be *saved* in our own strength; but the grace of God that saves us also teaches us to deny things that are ungodly and hold fast to that which is good, all the while looking for "that blessed hope," the glorious appearing of Jesus!

There is a definite connection between the *grace of God and CHRISTIAN STEWARDSHIP.*

Paul urged the believers in Rome to present themselves "a living sacrifice" unto God. This, he declared, is *the reasonable service* of a believer. He also besought them not to be *conformed to this world,* but rather to be *transformed* by the renewing of the mind, proving "what is that good, and acceptable, and perfect will of God.

"For I say, through the grace given unto me, to every man that is among you, not to think of himself more highly than he ought to think; but to think soberly, according as God hath dealt to every man the measure of faith. For as we have many members in one body, and all members have not the same office: so we, being many, are one body in Christ, and every one members one of another.

"Having then gifts differing according to the grace that is given to us, whether prophecy, let us prophesy according to the proportion of faith. Or ministry, let us wait on our ministering. Or he that teacheth, on teaching. Or he that exhorteth, on exhortation. He that giveth, let him do it with simplicity; he that ruleth, with diligence; he that sheweth mercy, with cheerfulness.

"Let love be without dissimulation. Abhor

that which is evil, cleave to that which is good. Be kindly affectioned one to another with brotherly love; in honour preferring one another; not slothful in business; fervent in spirit, serving the Lord; rejoicing in hope; patient in tribulation; continuing instant in prayer; distributing to the necessity of saints; given to hospitality.

"Bless them which persecute you: bless, and curse not. Rejoice with them that do rejoice, and weep with them that weep. Be of the same mind one toward another. Mind not high things, but condescend to men of low estate. Be not wise in your own conceits. Recompense to no man evil for evil. Provide things honest in the sight of all men. If it be possible, as much as lieth in you, live peaceably with all men.

"Dearly beloved, avenge not yourselves, but rather give place unto wrath: for it is written, Vengeance is mine; I will repay, saith the Lord. Therefore if thine enemy hunger, feed him; if he thirst, give him drink: for in so doing thou shalt heap coals of fire on his head. Be not overcome of evil, but overcome evil with good" (Rom. 12: 1-21).

I Peter 4:10 instructs, "As every man hath received the gift, even so minister the same one to another, *as good stewards of the manifold GRACE OF GOD.*"

The Word of God clearly teaches that the only possible way to grow in the spiritual life and in the knowledge of Christ is *by GRACE:*

"For our rejoicing is this, the testimony of our conscience, that in simplicity and godly sincerity, *not with fleshly wisdom, but by THE GRACE OF GOD*, we have had our conversation in the world, and more abundantly to you-ward" (II Cor. 1:12).

"Let no corrupt communication proceed out of your mouth, but that which is good to the use of edifying, *that it may minister GRACE unto the hearers*" (Eph. 4:29).

"Let the Word of Christ dwell in you richly in all wisdom; teaching and admonishing one another in psalms and hymns and spiritual songs, singing *with GRACE in your hearts* to the Lord" (Col. 3:16).

"Let your speech be *alway with GRACE*, seasoned with salt, that ye may know how ye ought to answer every man" (Col. 4:6).

"That the name of our Lord Jesus Christ may be glorified in you, and ye in Him, *according to the GRACE of our God and the Lord Jesus Christ*" (II Thess. 1:12).

"Let us therefore come boldly unto *the throne of GRACE*, that we may obtain mercy, and find *GRACE to help in time of need*" (Heb. 4:16).

"Wherefore we receiving a kingdom which cannot be moved, *let us have GRACE, whereby we may serve God acceptably* with reverence and godly fear: for our God is a consuming fire" (Heb. 12:28, 29).

Grace also has to do with CHRISTIAN GIV-ING:

During the Old Testament economy, people were commanded to pay a tithe, and they were declared to be "robbers" when they failed to bring all their tithes into the storehouse. I believe tithing is a good rule to follow, but we should never say that we *"pay"* a tithe, because in this Christian era we do not "pay." *We GIVE as we love Jesus*— not of necessity, but out of a heart of love and thanksgiving.

In II Corinthians 8:12-14 Paul speaks of the collection for the needy saints in other churches, and then exhorts the Corinthian believers to share their giving with those who were less fortunate:

"For if there be first a willing mind, it is accepted according to that a man hath, and not according to that he hath not. For I mean not that other men be eased, and ye burdened: but by an equality, that now at this time your abundance may be a supply for their want, that their abundance also may be a supply for your want: that there may be equality."

In II Corinthians chapters 8 and 9, Paul sums up the doctrine of Christian giving in this Dispensation of Grace. (I trust you will read those two chapters, since time and space will not permit quoting of the entire text here.)

Giving is a *grace*—that is, *the desire to give* is created in the heart by the Holy Spirit. He leads us as to what to give and where to give it. During the Dispensation of Law, giving was imposed upon the people as a divine command; but in *this* dispensation, giving is voluntary and is prompted by sincere love to God. Giving is a universal privilege among believers *according to the ability of the individual to give.* The rich can give much, the poor may give little. But God does not look upon the size of the gift—He looks upon the heart that prompted the giving.

The New Testament clearly teaches that Christian giving is to be proportioned according to an individual's income. Paul instructed the church at Corinth, "Upon the first day of the week let every one of you lay by him in store, *as God hath PROSPERED him,* that there be no gatherings when I come" (I Cor. 16:2).

To practice the grace of giving brings peculiar joy to the heart of the believer because he has a part in the ministry of the Gospel, spreading the good news of salvation and helping those who are less fortunate than himself: "Moreover, brethren, we do you to wit of the grace of God bestowed on the churches of Macedonia; how that in a great trial of affliction the abundance of their joy and their deep poverty abounded unto the riches of their liberality" (II Cor. 8:1, 2).

It is also true that *the more we give,* the more God gives us *to* give. This is a Bible promise:

"This I say: He which soweth sparingly shall

reap also sparingly; and he which soweth bountifully shall reap also bountifully. Every man according as he purposeth in his heart, so let him give; not grudgingly, or of necessity: for God loveth a cheerful giver. And God is able to make all grace abound toward you; that ye, always having all sufficiency in all things, may abound to every good work: (As it is written, He hath dispersed abroad; He hath given to the poor: His righteousness remaineth for ever. Now He that ministereth seed to the sower both minister bread for your food, and multiply your seed sown, and increase the fruits of your righteousness;) being enriched in every thing to all bountifulness, which causeth through us thanksgiving to God" (II Cor. 9:6-11).

The more we give, the greater our own capacity for thanksgiving to God for our own blessings: "For the administration of this service not only supplieth the want of the saints, but is abundant also by many thanksgivings unto God" (II Cor. 9:12).

When we give abundantly—heaped up, pressed down, and running over—we glorify God, and the Gospel message is sent to the ends of the earth: "Whiles by the experiment of this ministration they glorify God for your professed subjection unto the Gospel of Christ, and for your liberal distribution unto them, and unto all men; and by their prayer for you, which long after you for the exceeding grace of God in you" (II Cor. 9:13, 14).

I firmly believe that one reason many believers do not have an abundance of this world's possessions is because they do not give out of a heart of love—cheerfully and liberally. If we are "stingy" toward God, He cannot trust us with an abundance of this world's goods; but if we give as we are prospered of the Lord, then He will prosper us even more. Do not misunderstand me—we do not give in order to prosper. We prosper because we give. And when we give in the true spirit we do not think of what we will receive in return.

Even our SPEECH is to be seasoned with GRACE: "Let your speech be *alway with GRACE,* seasoned with salt, that ye may know how ye ought to answer every man" (Col. 4:6). Most believers need to study and commit to memory the words of Jesus in Matthew 12:33-37:

"Either make the tree good, and his fruit good; or else make the tree corrupt, and his fruit corrupt: for the tree is known by his fruit. O generation of vipers, how can ye, being evil, speak good things? for out of the abundance of the heart the mouth speaketh. A good man out of the good treasure of the heart bringeth forth good things: and an evil man out of the evil treasure bringeth forth evil things. But I say unto you, That *EVERY IDLE WORD that men shall speak, they shall give account thereof in the day of judgment. For BY THY WORDS thou shalt be justified, and by thy WORDS thou shalt be condemned."*

Christians should be very careful of the language they use and the manner in which they speak. James declares, "If any man among you seem to be religious, *and bridleth not his TONGUE,* but deceiveth his own heart, this man's religion is vain" (James 1:26). So, according to this statement, the man who has a loose tongue also has a loose (or vain) religion! He does not have the grace of God in his heart.

James further declares, "For in many things we offend all. If any man *offend not in WORD,* the same is a perfect man, and able also to bridle the whole body" (James 3:2). This is a tremendous truth! The man who can control his words has the ability to control all other members of his body. How important it is that we, by the grace of God, set a guard at our lips, bridle our tongue, and speak not words of bitterness which will bring heartache and discord among Christians, or destroy our testimony before the unsaved!

In James 3:5-10 we read these words: "The tongue is a little member, and boasteth great things. Behold, how great a matter a little fire kindleth! And the tongue is a fire, a world of iniquity: so is the tongue among our members, that it defileth the whole body, and setteth on fire the course of nature; and it is set on fire of hell.

"For every kind of beasts, and of birds, and of

serpents, and of things in the sea, is tamed, and hath been tamed of mankind: but the tongue can no man tame; it is an unruly evil, full of deadly poison. Therewith bless we God, even the Father; and therewith curse we men, which are made after the similitude of God. Out of the same mouth proceedeth blessing and cursing. *My brethren, these things ought not so to be!*"

While the tongue can be a deadly instrument of evil, it can also be a sanctified servant of God. If the tongue is sanctified by grace and controlled by the Spirit of God, then it sends forth words of sweetness—helpful words, good conversation which is commendable to the Lord. "Who is a wise man and endued with knowledge among you? Let him shew out of a good conversation his works with meekness of wisdom" (James 3:13).

A *sanctified tongue* is compared to the following:—

1. *Silver*—for choiceness, value, and beauty: "The tongue of *the just* is as choice silver: the heart of the wicked is little worth" (Prov. 10:20).

2. *Food*—to strengthen: "The lips of *the righteous* feed many: but fools die for want of wisdom" (Prov. 10:21).

3. *Wholesome fruit*—to satisfy: "A man shall be satisfied with good by the fruit of his mouth: and the recompence of a man's hands shall be rendered unto him" (Prov. 12:14).

4. *Health*—to make one happy and gladden the heart: "There is that speaketh like the piercings of a sword: but *the tongue of the wise* is health" (Prov. 12:18).

5. *A tree of life*—to feed: "A wholesome tongue is a tree of life: but perverseness therein is a breach in the spirit" (Prov. 15:4).

6. *Honey*—to sweeten the soul: "Pleasant words are as an honeycomb, sweet to the soul, and health to the bones" (Prov. 16:24).

7. *A well-spring of water*—to cool and refresh: "The words of a man's mouth are as deep waters, and the well-spring of wisdom as a flowing brook" (Prov. 18:4).

8. *A jewel*—to beautify: "There is gold, and a multitude of rubies: but the lips of knowledge are a precious jewel" (Prov. 20:15).

9. *An object to admire:* "A word fitly spoken is like apples of gold in pictures of silver" (Prov. 25:11).

10. *A treasure*—to enrich: "A good man out of the good treasure of his heart bringeth forth that which is good; and an evil man out of the evil treasure of his heart bringeth forth that which is evil: for of the abundance of the heart his mouth speaketh" (Luke 6:45).

We need add only one letter to w-o-r-d-s to make it s-w-o-r-d-s—but what a difference between the two! It is not always *what* we say that hurts, but *how we say it.* Therefore as children of God and lights in a dark world let us mark well what we say and how we say it. We should pray with David, "Let the WORDS of my mouth, and the meditation of my HEART, be acceptable in thy sight, O Lord, my strength, and my Redeemer!" (Psalm 19:14).

Believers are looking for the grace which is to be revealed when Jesus comes for His Church: "Wherefore gird up the loins of your mind; be sober, and hope to the end for *the grace that is to be brought unto you at the revelation of Jesus Christ"* (I Pet. 1:13).

In verses 4 and 5 of this same chapter Peter speaks of "an inheritance incorruptible, and undefiled, and that fadeth not away, reserved in heaven for you, who are kept by the power of God through faith unto *salvation ready to be revealed in the last time."* This speaks of the salvation of the body, not the redemption of the soul. The soul is redeemed the moment we believe in Jesus, but we look forward to that blessed, happy morning when Jesus will come for His own and we will receive a body like unto His glorious resurrection body.

Grace IN CHRIST JESUS does indeed have many traits, and various are the things to which grace may be compared. We have by no means exhausted the subject here. We have just given a little taste of the marvelous grace of God, and what it does for the believer. We are saved by God's grace *through faith plus nothing,* and the grace that saves us also sustains us, establishes us, and is sufficient for any and all needs. The grace of God is the preserving power of God. It gives victory because it teaches us to deny ungodliness and worldly lusts, and to live soberly, righteously, and godly in this present world, looking for Jesus—and if we are looking for Jesus we will certainly not be living in the lust of the flesh!

The grace of God that *saves* us also *teaches* us to live for Jesus in this sinful world, *looking for His coming*—and the grace of God will lead us *home*:

> *Amazing grace! how sweet the sound,*
> *That saved a wretch like me!*
> *I once was lost, but now am found,*
> *Was blind, but now I see.*
>
> *'Twas grace that taught my heart to fear,*
> *And grace my fears relieved;*
> *How precious did that grace appear*
> *The hour I first believed!*
>
> *Through many dangers, toils and snares,*
> *I have already come;*
> *'Tis grace hath brought me safe thus far,*
> *And grace will lead me home.*
>
> *When we've been there ten thousand years,*
> *Bright shining as the sun,*
> *We've no less days to sing God's praise*
> *Than when we first begun.*

—John Newton

V
"Salvation... In Christ Jesus With Eternal Glory"

"Therefore I endure all things for the elect's sakes, that they may also obtain *the SALVATION which is IN CHRIST JESUS with eternal glory*" (II Tim. 2:10).

The salvation we possess in Christ is in three tenses—past, present, and future. We are saved from the *penalty* of sin the moment we believe on Jesus. We are delivered from the *power* of sin day by day, by God's grace. Then when Jesus comes in the Rapture and the first resurrection we will be saved from the very *presence* of sin and from the sphere of evil. It is this future "salvation" to which our present verse refers.

"*Salvation*" is a marvelous and inclusive word of the Gospel. In it are included all of the redemptive acts and processes—justification, redemption, grace, propitiation, imputation, forgiveness, sanctification, and (finally) glorification. We are told that the Hebrew and Greek words translated "salvation" imply deliverance, safety, preservation, soundness, and healing. Now let us look more closely at *the three tenses* of salvation:

Past:—

The believer *has been saved* (redeemed) from the guilt and penalty of sin. Luke 7:36-50 gives the account of the Lord's visit to the home of Simon the Pharisee. During His visit there, a very wicked

107

woman came in, bringing "an alabaster box of ointment, and stood at His feet . . . weeping, and began to wash His feet with tears, and did wipe them with the hairs of her head, and kissed His feet, and anointed them with the ointment." Simon "spake within himself, saying, This Man, if He were a prophet, would have known who and what manner of woman this is that toucheth Him: for she is a sinner." Jesus therefore gave Simon the Pharisee a lesson in forgiveness, and then said to the woman, "Thy faith *HATH SAVED thee.* Go in peace."

Notice Jesus used the past tense of salvation— *"saved"*—not a process, but an act accomplished, *completed.* Redemption is instantaneous. We are redeemed from the penalty of sin which would damn the soul. In II Timothy 1:9 Paul speaks of God having *"saved us* (past tense) and called us with an holy calling . . . according to His own purpose and grace . . . ."

I Peter 2:24 tells us that Christ "His own self *BARE our sins* (past tense) in His own body on the tree, that we, being dead to sins, should live unto righteousness: by whose stripes *ye WERE HEALED."* Christ *bore* our sins. He is not now bearing, He has *already borne,* our sins, and by His stripes we *were healed.* We were redeemed, we were healed, the very moment we believed on Jesus.
Present:—

Believers are also *saved daily* from the *power*

(habit or dominion) *of sin.* When God saves from the penalty of sin He saves with a perfect salvation and the saved one need never pray the sinner's prayer again. However, we do need to pray that God will deliver us from evil (Matt. 6:13), direct us "in paths of righteousness for His name's sake" (Psalm 23:3), and show us the way of escape from temptation: "There hath no temptation taken you but such as is common to man: but God is faithful, who will not suffer you to be tempted above that ye are able; but will with the temptation also make *a way to escape,* that ye may be able to bear it" (I Cor. 10:13).

There are some people who say, "If I *hold ON,* God is able to *hold OUT."* This is fallacy. We are not able to hold on *or* hold out. We are kept by the power of Almighty God:

"Blessed be the God and Father of our Lord Jesus Christ, which according to His abundant mercy hath begotten us again unto a lively hope by the resurrection of Jesus Christ from the dead, to an inheritance incorruptible, and undefiled, and that fadeth not away, reserved in heaven for you, *who are KEPT by the power of God* through faith unto salvation ready to be revealed in the last time" (I Pet. 1:3-5).

Romans 6:14 tells us, "Sin *shall not* have dominion over you: for ye are not under the law, but under *grace."*

Paul assured the Philippians, ". . . He which

hath *begun* a good work in you *will perform it* until the day of Jesus Christ" (Phil. 1:6).

Romans 8:37 gives us assurance that *in all things* "we are *more than conquerors* through Him that loved us."

In Ephesians 4:30 we read, "Grieve not the Holy Spirit of God, whereby ye are *sealed unto the day of redemption."* This, too, speaks of redemption of the *body,* not salvation of the soul, for certainly the Holy Spirit would not *dwell* in the heart of an unsaved person.

Future:—

When Jesus returns in the Rapture, born again believers will be saved from *the very presence of sin.* We will be taken out of sin's domain, caught up out of the kingdom of Satan, to meet Jesus in the clouds in the air. The spirits of believers who die before the Rapture will be resting with Jesus— to be absent from the body is to be present with the Lord (Phil. 1:23; II Cor. 5:6); but in the Rapture and the first resurrection the bodies of the saints will be raised and the living saints will be caught up with them, to meet Jesus. It is then that we will be saved in the sense of entire conformity to Christ, and we will be like Him.

Paul explains it in these words:

"Behold, I shew you a mystery: We shall not all sleep, but we shall all be changed, in a moment, in the twinkling of an eye, at the last trump:

for the trumpet shall sound, and the dead shall be raised incorruptible, and we shall be changed. For this corruptible must put on incorruption, and this mortal must put on immortality. So when this corruptible shall have put on incorruption, and this mortal shall have put on immortality, then shall be brought to pass the saying that is written, Death is swallowed up in victory.

"O death, where is thy sting? O grave, where is thy victory? The sting of death is sin; and the strength of sin is the law. But thanks be to God, which giveth us the victory through our Lord Jesus Christ" (I Cor. 15:51-57).

To the Thessalonian believers Paul wrote:

"The Lord Himself shall descend from heaven with a shout, with the voice of the archangel, and with the trump of God: and the dead in Christ shall rise first. Then we which are alive and remain shall be caught up together with them in the clouds, to meet the Lord in the air: and so shall we ever be with the Lord. Wherefore comfort one another with these words" (I Thess. 4:16-18).

In Romans 13:11 we are told that "it is high time to awake out of sleep: for *now is our salvation nearer than when we believed"*—again speaking of the future, the salvation of the body at the return of the Lord Jesus Christ.

Many believers need to realize that *Christians possess eternal life NOW*, we are *delivered from condemnation NOW.* John 3:36 tells us, "He that

111

believeth on the Son *HATH* (present tense) *everlasting life . . . .*" In John 5:24 Jesus Himself declared, "He that heareth my Word, and believeth on Him that sent me, *HATH* (now) *everlasting life,* and shall not come into condemnation; but *IS PASSED from death unto life.*" It is not a matter of the believer's *having eternal life when he dies or when Jesus comes.* Eternal life becomes ours the second we believe on Jesus unto salvation. We pass from spiritual deadness to spiritual life, and from that moment until we reach Paradise we *possess* eternal life. The *inner man* is eternally saved, and the *body* will be made new at the first resurrection.

The believer's expectation, then, is expressed in these words: "Our conversation (citizenship) is in heaven, from whence also we look for the Saviour, the Lord Jesus Christ: *who shall change our vile BODY, that it may be fashioned like unto His glorious body,* according to the working whereby He is able even to subdue all things unto Himself" (Phil. 3:20, 21).

We sit together with Jesus in heavenly places *now* (Eph. 2:6), and we will be redeemed *in body* in that glorious morning when Jesus saves us from the presence of sin. "For we know that the whole creation groaneth and travaileth in pain together until now. And not only they, but ourselves also, which have the firstfruits of the Spirit, even we ourselves groan within ourselves, *waiting for the*

adoption, to wit, the REDEMPTION of our BODY"
(Rom. 8:22, 23).

VI
"Godliness . . . In Christ Jesus"

"Yea, and all that will *live godly in Christ Jesus* shall suffer persecution" (II Tim. 3:12).

"And without controversy great is *the mystery of godliness:* God was manifest in the flesh, justified in the Spirit, seen of angels, preached unto the Gentiles, believed on in the world, received up into glory" (I Tim. 3:16).

The "mystery" here is the mystery of God manifest in the flesh—that is, *Jesus was God in flesh:*

"In the beginning was the Word, and the Word was with God, and the Word was God. . . . And the Word was made flesh, and dwelt among us, (and we beheld His glory, the glory as of the only begotten of the Father,) full of grace and truth" (John 1:1, 14).

This does not destroy the doctrine of the Trinity —one God manifest in three Persons—Father, Son, and Holy Ghost. When Philip said to Jesus, "Lord, shew us the Father, and it sufficeth us," Jesus replied: "Have I been so long time with you, and yet *hast thou not known me, Philip? He that hath seen ME hath seen the FATHER:* and how sayest thou then, Shew us the Father?" (John 14:8, 9).

In John 10:30 Jesus plainly declared, *"I and my*

Father are ONE."

In I John 1:5 we read, ". . . *God is LIGHT, and in Him is no darkness at all."* Jesus said, "As long as I am *in* the world, I am *the LIGHT* of the world" (John 9:5). Jesus is now seated at the right hand of the Majesty on high, but we are His children, we possess divine nature; and since we are children of God we are also children of light, children of the day (I Thess. 5:5). "For ye were sometimes darkness, but now are ye *light in the Lord:* walk as *children of light"* (Eph. 5:8). Jesus told His disciples, "Ye are the light of the world. . . . Let your light so shine before men, that they may see your good works, and glorify your Father which is in heaven" (Matt. 5:14, 16).

Jesus was God manifest in the flesh, and He is the One who can make God manifest *in US.* Only the brightness *of* God's glory can make us bright *with* God's glory. Divine nature in the inner man shines forth in what we do, in what we say, and in every detail of our lives. The world watches believers. Unbelievers look upon us as God's representatives. Paul said to the believers in Corinth, "Ye are our epistle written in our hearts, *known and read* of all men: forasmuch as ye are manifestly declared to be the epistle of Christ ministered by us, written not with ink, but with the Spirit of the living God; not in tables of stone, but in fleshy tables of the heart" (II Cor. 3:2, 3).

Jesus is the brightness of God's glory, the express

image of His Person (Heb. 1:3), and He can stamp *us* with the Father's image. We are to exalt Christ in all godliness of life, speech, and company. It is our duty—as well as our privilege—to glorify God through godliness! The Lord Jesus, abiding in our hearts in the Person of the Holy Spirit, can reproduce in us the beauty of Himself—and it is *only IN HIM* that we can display godliness. "But we all, with open face beholding as in a glass the glory of the Lord, are changed *into the same image* from glory to glory, even as by the Spirit of the Lord" (II Cor. 3:18).

In his letter to the Ephesian believers Paul describes the believer's position in grace:

"Blessed be the God and Father of our Lord Jesus Christ, who hath blessed us with all spiritual blessings in heavenly places in Christ: according as He hath *chosen us IN HIM before the foundation of the world, that we should be HOLY and WITHOUT BLAME before Him in love:* having predestinated us unto the adoption of children by Jesus Christ to Himself, according to the good pleasure of His will, to the praise of the glory of His grace, wherein He hath made us *accepted IN THE BELOVED.* In whom we have redemption through His blood, the forgiveness of sins, according to the riches of His grace; wherein He hath abounded toward us in all wisdom and prudence; having made known unto us the mystery of His will, according to His good pleasure which

He hath purposed in Himself: That in the dispensation of the fulness of times *He might gather together in one ALL THINGS IN CHRIST*, both which are in heaven, and which are on earth; even in Him: in whom also we have obtained an inheritance, being predestinated according to the purpose of Him who worketh all things after the counsel of His own will: that we should be to the praise of His glory, who first trusted in Christ.

"In whom ye also trusted, after that ye heard the Word of truth, the Gospel of your salvation: in whom also after that ye believed, ye were sealed with that Holy Spirit of promise, which is the earnest of our inheritance until the redemption of the purchased possession, unto the praise of His glory.

"Wherefore I also, after I heard of your faith in the Lord Jesus, and love unto all the saints, cease not to give thanks for you, making mention of you in my prayers; that the God of our Lord Jesus Christ, the Father of glory, may give unto you the spirit of wisdom and revelation in the knowledge of Him: the eyes of your understanding being enlightened; that ye may know what is the hope of His calling, and what the riches of the glory of His inheritance in the saints, and what is the exceeding greatness of His power to us-ward who believe, according to the working of His mighty power, which He wrought in Christ when He raised Him from the dead, and set Him at

His own right hand in the heavenly places, far above all principality, and power, and might, and dominion, and every name that is named, not only in this world, but also in that which is to come: and hath put all things under His feet, and gave Him to be the head over all things to the Church, which is His body, the fulness of Him that filleth all in all" (Eph. 1:3-23).

The Scriptures clearly teach that God saves us for Christ's sake. We are God's children by grace, and as His children we should display godliness in our lives in all that we are and in all that we do. This we should do to the glory and praise of our God who loved us so much.

To Timothy Paul wrote, "I exhort therefore, that, first of all, supplications, prayers, intercessions, and giving of thanks, be made for all men; for kings, and for all that are in authority; that we may lead a quiet and peaceable life in all godliness and honesty. For this is good and acceptable in the sight of God our Saviour, who will have all men to be saved, and to come unto the knowledge of the truth. *For there is ONE GOD, and ONE MEDIATOR BETWEEN GOD AND MEN, the Man Christ Jesus,* who gave Himself a ransom for all, to be testified in due time" (I Tim. 2:1-6).

Paul further exhorted Timothy, "Refuse profane and old wives' fables, and exercise thyself rather *unto GODLINESS.* For bodily exercise profiteth little: but *GODLINESS is profitable unto all things*, having promise of the life that now is, and of that which is to come" (I Tim. 4:7, 8).

So we see that a quiet, peaceable life, lived in all godliness and honesty, is acceptable in the sight of God, and through such living men will see Christ magnified in us.

Then in I Timothy 6:1-16 Paul continues: "Let as many servants as are under the yoke count their own masters worthy of all honour, that the name of God and His doctrine be not blasphemed. And they that have believing masters, let them not despise them, because they are brethren; but rather do them service, because they are faithful and beloved, partakers of the benefit.   These things teach and exhort.

"If any man teach otherwise, and consent not to wholesome words, even the words of our Lord Jesus Christ, and to the doctrine which is according to godliness; he is proud, knowing nothing, but doting about questions and strifes of words, whereof cometh envy, strife, railings, evil surmisings, perverse disputings of men of corrupt minds, and destitute of the truth, supposing that gain is godliness: from such withdraw thyself.

"But godliness with contentment is great gain. For we brought nothing into this world, and it is certain we can carry nothing out.   And having food and raiment let us be therewith content. But they that will be rich fall into temptation and a snare, and into many foolish and hurtful lusts, which drown men in destruction and perdition. For the love of money is the root of all evil: which while some coveted after, they have erred from the faith, and pierced themselves through with many sorrows.

"But thou, O man of God, flee these things; and follow after righteousness, godliness, faith, love, patience, meekness. Fight the good fight of faith, lay hold on eternal life, whereunto thou art also called, and hast professed a good profession before many witnesses. I give thee charge in the sight of God, who quickeneth all things, and before Christ Jesus, who before Pontius Pilate witnessed a good confession; that thou keep this commandment without spot, unrebukeable, until the appearing of our Lord Jesus Christ: which in His times He shall shew, who is the blessed and only Potentate, the King of kings, and Lord of lords; who only hath immortality, dwelling in the light which no man can approach unto; whom no man hath seen, nor can see: to whom be honour and power everlasting. Amen."

To the young minister Titus, Paul wrote: "Paul, a servant of God, and an apostle of Jesus Christ, according to the faith of God's elect, and the acknowledging of *the truth which is after GOD-LINESS*; in hope of eternal life, which God, that cannot lie, promised before the world began; but hath in due times manifested His Word through preaching, which is committed unto me according to the commandment of God our Saviour; to Titus, mine own son after the common faith: Grace, mercy, and peace, from God the Father and the Lord Jesus Christ our Saviour" (Tit. 1:1-4).

The Apostle Peter also preached godliness: "Simon Peter, a servant and an apostle of Jesus Christ, to them that have obtained like precious faith with us through the righteousness of God and our Saviour Jesus Christ: Grace and peace be multiplied unto you through the knowledge of God, and of Jesus our Lord, according as His divine power hath given unto us *all things that pertain unto life and GODLINESS*, through the knowledge of Him that hath called us to glory and virtue: whereby are given unto us exceeding great and precious promises: that by these ye might be partakers of the divine nature, having escaped the corruption that is in the world through lust.

"And beside this, giving all diligence, add to your faith virtue; and to virtue knowledge; and to knowledge temperance; and to temperance patience; *and to patience GODLINESS;* and to godliness brotherly kindness; and to brotherly kindness charity. For if these things be in you, and abound, they make you that ye shall neither be barren nor unfruitful in the knowledge of our Lord Jesus Christ" (II Pet. 1:1-8).

Speaking of the time to come when "the heavens

shall pass away with a great noise, and the elements shall melt with fervent heat, the earth also and the works that are therein shall be burned up," Peter then asks: "Seeing then that all these things shall be dissolved, what manner of persons ought ye to be *in all holy conversation and GODLINESS*, looking for and hasting unto the coming of the day of God, wherein the heavens being on fire shall be dissolved, and the elements shall melt with fervent heat?" (II Pet. 3:10-12).

VII
"Faith . . . In Christ Jesus"

"Continue thou in the things which thou hast learned and hast been assured of, knowing of whom thou hast learned them; and that from a child thou hast known the holy Scriptures, which are able to make thee wise unto salvation *through FAITH which is in Christ Jesus*" (II Tim. 3:14, 15).

We are saved by grace, *pure grace,* apart from works. Saving grace becomes ours through faith—but where do we get the faith with which to appropriate grace?

Hebrews 11:6 tells us that *without faith* it is impossible to please God, and faith to appropriate saving grace is found *only IN CHRIST*. He is the door to heaven (John 10:9), He is "the Way, the Truth, and the Life" (John 14:6). "Neither is there salvation in any other: for there is none other name under heaven given among men, whereby we must be saved" (Acts 4:12). So then—*Jesus is the grace that saves,* and He is also *the faith* that appropriates grace. All spiritual blessings— faith, grace, redemption, salvation, righteousness, propitiation, forgiveness, sanctification, holiness— are ours in Jesus, and *apart from Him there IS no spiritual blessing!*

Jesus brought grace down to man, but He also brought *faith* down to men in order that we might *receive* saving grace. The Gospel of the Lord Jesus Christ "is the power of God unto salvation to every one that believeth . . . for therein is the righteousness of God revealed from faith to faith: as it is written, *The just shall live by faith*" (Rom. 1:16, 17). Thus we see that the very *faith* through which we receive the gift of God and appropriate saving grace is *also* God's gift.

"But now the righteousness of God without the law is manifested, being witnessed by the law and the prophets; even *the righteousness of God which is BY FAITH of Jesus Christ* unto all and upon all them that believe . . ." (Rom. 3:21, 22).

"For what saith the Scripture? *Abraham believed God,* and it was counted unto him for righteousness. Now to him that worketh is the reward not reckoned of grace, but of debt. But to him that worketh not, but believeth on Him that justifieth the ungodly, *his FAITH is counted for righteousness*" (Rom. 4:3-5).

Faith in Christ is counted for righteousness,

Christ "is made unto us righteousness" (I Cor. 1:30), therefore Christ gives faith to appropriate righteousness—God's gift entirely apart from works.

In John 1:18 we read, "No man hath seen God at any time. The only begotten Son, which is in the bosom of the Father, *He hath DECLARED Him.*" In living words, wonderful words of life, Jesus declared God's love, mercy, and grace. He said, *"The WORDS that I speak unto you, they are spirit, and they are life"* (John 6:63). He said, *"He that heareth MY WORD,* and believeth on Him that sent me, hath everlasting life, and shall not come into condemnation; but is passed from death unto life" (John 5:24).

The words Jesus spoke, words recorded in our Bible, bring faith that appropriates saving grace: *"So then FAITH cometh by HEARING, and hearing by THE WORD OF GOD"* (Rom. 10:17).

Not only are we saved by grace through faith, but the Christian life *continues* in faith—"the just shall *LIVE by faith"* (Rom. 1:17). This simply means that the believer lives *on faith*. Jesus said, "I am that bread of life. Your fathers did eat manna in the wilderness, and are dead. This is the bread which cometh down from heaven, that a man may eat thereof, and not die.

"I am the living bread which came down from heaven. If any man eat of this bread, he shall live for ever: and the bread that I will give is my flesh, which I will give for the life of the world....

"Verily, verily, I say unto you, Except ye eat the flesh of the Son of man, and drink His blood, ye have no life in you. Whoso eateth my flesh, and drinketh my blood, hath eternal life; and I will raise him up at the last day. For my flesh is meat indeed, and my blood is drink indeed. He that eateth my flesh, and drinketh my blood, dwelleth in me, and I in him. As the living Father hath sent me, and I live by the Father: so he that eateth me, even he shall live by me.

"This is that bread which came down from heaven: not as your fathers did eat manna, and are dead: he that eateth of this bread shall live for ever. . . . It is the Spirit that quickeneth; the flesh profiteth nothing. The WORDS that I speak unto you, they are spirit, and they are LIFE" (John 6:48-63 in part).

So when Jesus said "Except ye eat the flesh of the Son of man, and drink His blood, ye have no life in you," He simply meant *"Except you eat* (appropriate) *the WORD,* you have no life in you." We are saved by grace through faith. Faith comes by hearing the Word, the Word brings faith to appropriate grace, and the Word furnishes spiritual food. Therefore "the just shall live by (or on) faith" (Hab. 2:4; Rom. 1:17; Gal. 3:11; Heb. 10:38).

God revealed to Paul that the Gentiles should be fellowheirs of the same body (the Church), and partakers of His promise in Christ by the Gospel, "to the intent that now unto the principalities and powers in heavenly places might be known by the Church the manifold wisdom of God, according to the eternal purpose which He purposed in Christ Jesus our Lord, in whom we have *boldness and access with confidence by THE FAITH OF HIM*" (Eph. 3:10-12).

So we have access into grace by faith: "Therefore being justified by faith, we have peace with God through our Lord Jesus Christ; by whom also we have *access by FAITH into this GRACE wherein we stand,* and rejoice in hope of the glory of God" (Rom. 5:1, 2).

God assured Paul, "My grace is sufficient for thee!" (II Cor. 12:9). By faith in Christ Jesus, all believers have access into this storehouse of grace. Victory over the world, the flesh, and the devil comes—not by might nor by power, not by "trying" nor "abstaining"—*but BY FAITH:* "For whatsoever is born of God *overcometh the world:* and this is the victory that overcometh the world, *even our FAITH*" (I John 5:4).

To the Galatian believers, Paul gave this testimony: "I am crucified with Christ: nevertheless *I live*—yet not I, but *CHRIST liveth in me:* and the life which I now live in the flesh I live *by the FAITH of the Son of God,* who loved me, and gave Himself for me" (Gal. 2:20).

I Peter 1:5 clearly teaches that we are *KEPT by faith*—"kept by the power of God *through FAITH* unto salvation ready to be revealed in the last time."

Jesus instructed His disciples, *"Have FAITH in God"* (Mark 11:22). It is true that *without* faith it is impossible to please God (Heb. 11:6), and it is equally true that "whatsoever is NOT of faith is SIN" (Rom. 14:23).

In this message we have seen that *the sphere of the believer is IN CHRIST JESUS*, and we have discussed seven distinct things which are found in Christ as we live and move and have our being in Him. Then in Paul's second letter to the Corinthian church we read:

"For God, who commanded the light to shine out of darkness, hath shined in our hearts, to give the light of the knowledge of the glory of God in the face of Jesus Christ. But we have this treasure in earthen vessels, that the excellency of the power may be of God, and not of us. . . .

"We having the same spirit of faith, according as it is written, I believed, and therefore have I spoken; we also believe, and therefore speak; knowing that He which raised up the Lord Jesus shall raise up us also by Jesus, and shall present us with you. For all things are for your sakes, that the abundant grace might through the thanksgiving of many redound to the glory of God. For which cause we faint not; but though our outward man perish, yet the inward man is renewed day by day. For our light affliction, which is but for a moment, worketh for us a far more exceeding and eternal weight of glory: while we look not at the things which are seen, but at the things which are not seen: for the things which are seen are temporal; but the things which are not seen are eternal" (II Cor. 4:6-18 in part).

Peter reassures us by telling us that "for a season, if need be, ye are in heaviness through manifold temptations: *that the trial of your faith, being much more precious than of gold that perisheth, though it be tried with fire, might be found unto praise and honour and glory at the appearing of Jesus Christ:* whom having not seen, ye love: in whom, though now ye see Him not, yet believing, ye rejoice with joy unspeakable and full of glory: receiving the end of your faith, even the salvation of your souls. . . . Wherefore gird up the loins of your mind, be sober, and hope to the end for the grace that is to be brought unto you at the revelation of Jesus Christ" (I Pet. 1:6-13 in part).

It is the sincere prayer of my heart that each and every believer who reads this message will be blessed, fed, strengthened, and encouraged through the Gospel.

I trust that *unbelievers* who may read these lines will be convicted of their need of Christ and will receive Him as Saviour this very moment. Remember, unsaved friend, God is "not willing that *any* should perish, *but that ALL should come to repentance"* (II Pet. 3:9).

His invitation is, *"Come unto me,* all ye that labour and are heavy laden, and I will give you rest" (Matt. 11:28).

His promise is, "Him that cometh to me *I will in no wise cast out"* (John 6:37).

John 1:12, 13 declares: "As many as received Him, to them gave He power to become the sons of God, even to them that believe on His name: which were born, not of blood, nor of the will of the flesh, nor of the will of man, but of God."

Romans 10:9, 10 explains: "If thou shalt confess with thy mouth the Lord Jesus, and shalt believe in thine heart that God hath raised Him from the dead, *thou shalt be SAVED.* For with the heart man believeth unto righteousness; and with the mouth confession is made unto salvation."

God has never broken a promise. He cannot lie (Tit. 1:2; Heb. 6:18). If you will confess your sins and ask Him to save you for Jesus' sake, He will save you—and you will know it, because He will give you the witness of the Holy Spirit in your heart (Rom. 8:16).

TWO BIRDS

Two Birds

"And the Lord spake unto Moses, saying: This shall be the law of the leper in the day of his cleansing: He shall be brought unto the priest, and the priest shall go forth out of the camp; and the priest shall look, and behold, if the plague of the leprosy be healed in the leper, then shall the priest command to take for him that is to be cleansed two birds alive and clean, and cedar wood, and scarlet, and hyssop: and the priest shall command that one of the birds be killed in an earthen vessel over running water. As for the living bird, he shall take it, and the cedar wood, and the scarlet, and the hyssop, and shall dip them and the living bird in the blood of the bird that was killed over the running water; and he shall sprinkle upon him that is to be cleansed from the leprosy seven times, and shall pronounce him clean, and shall let the living bird loose into the open field" (Lev. 14:1-7).

This passage presents one of the most striking, most beautiful pictures of salvation to be found in the Old Testament. The verses quoted here speak, literally, of the law for the cleansing of a leper; but in the Word of God, *leprosy* is a type of sin and the leper is a type of the sinner. Jesus came into the world for the specific purpose of saving sinners by cleansing them from sin.

For the leper who was to be cleansed, the priest was to take *"two birds alive and clean . . . ."* Some commentators tell us that these birds were sparrows. The literal rendering is "little birds." The sparrow is a small and insignificant bird, weak and humble, very inexpensive if bought on the market. In Matthew 10:29 Jesus spoke of sparrows as selling two for a *farthing*—or one-fourth of a penny!

We can make a significant comparison here: As the sparrow is an insignificant, humble bird, so Jesus in His earthly life was humble and insignificant before those whom He came to save. Isaiah 53:2, 3 gives this description of Him:

"He shall grow up before Him as a tender plant, and as a root out of a dry ground: He hath no form nor comeliness; and when we shall see Him, there is no beauty that we should desire Him. He is despised and rejected of men; a Man of sorrows, and acquainted with grief: and we hid as it were our faces from Him. He was despised, and we esteemed Him not."

The Jews would not accept this humble King to reign over them. They were looking for a mighty man of valor, a conquering hero who would deliver them from the yoke of pagan Rome and re-establish the former glory of Israel. So even though their prophets had identified the Messiah *in detail,* the Jews failed to recognize Him.

But there are still more comparisons to be made, more "types and shadows" to be seen, in our Scripture text from Leviticus 14:

1. There were *two birds.*

This sets forth the twofoldness of Christ. He was from heaven (John 3:13), and He was also of earth—"the *Man* Christ Jesus" (I Tim. 2:5). Jesus was God in flesh (II Cor. 5:19), therefore He was the *God-man.*

2. The birds must be *"alive and clean."*

This shows forth Jesus, the Author of life, and His sinlessness. He "was in all points tempted like as we are, yet without sin" (Heb. 4:15). There was no sin in Jesus. He came into the world to take *the sin of the world* upon Himself; and even though He did just that and finished the work He came to do, He was nevertheless alive and holy, as the two birds used in the cleansing of the leper were to be "alive and clean."

3. The priest was to use *"cedar wood."*

There are several peculiarities about cedar. In the first place, the *heart* of cedar never decays. A cedar post set into the ground will, in time, deteriorate on the outside, but the red heart of the cedar will not decay. Jesus was flesh from the standpoint of man, but His blood came from God (Acts 20:28). His flesh could die—but never the inner Man.

Cedar wood is also *fragrant*. This, too, is typical of Jesus who "hath given Himself for us an offering and a sacrifice to God *for a sweetsmelling savour*" (Eph. 5:2).

4. ". . . *and scarlet.*"

Yes, there had to be scarlet in the cleansing. Rahab the harlot was told to bind a line of scarlet thread in her window, that she and her family might be spared when the Israelites took the land. (Read Joshua 2:1-22 for the account of Rahab and the spies whose lives were saved because of her help.)

God still demands scarlet, and without it there can be no forgiveness—"without shedding of blood is no remission" (Heb. 9:22). We are "not redeemed with corruptible things, as silver and gold . . . but with the precious blood of Christ, as of a lamb without blemish and without spot" (I Pet. 1:18, 19), and "the blood of Jesus Christ (God's) Son cleanseth us from all sin" (I John 1:7). The *scarlet* must be there. God still thunders out, *"When I see the BLOOD, I will pass over you!"* (Ex. 12:13).

5. ". . . *and hyssop.*"

Hyssop is the weakest of plants. It grows on

rocks and clings to the rock for life and sustenance. Here, hyssop represents *faith*. In *itself*, faith is nothing; but it is the *nexus* between need and supply, the link between weakness and strength. As the hyssop, bound to the cedar wood with scarlet twine, was the instrumentality for application of the blood, so is faith. That is, we are saved by *grace*, grace was made possible by *blood*, and *faith applies the blood*. We must approach God through faith, and "*without* faith it is impossible to please Him" (Heb. 11:6). So as hyssop (the *weakest* of nature) depends on the rock (the *strongest* of nature), so weak, helpless mankind must have faith in the Rock, Christ Jesus, if we hope to enter heaven. "Whosoever shall fall upon that Stone shall be broken; but on whomsoever it shall fall, it will grind him to powder!" (Luke 20:18).

6. The bird must be killed *outside the camp.*

This, too, was typical of the death of the Lord Jesus Christ. "Wherefore Jesus also, that He might sanctify the people with His own blood, suffered without the gate" (Heb. 13:12). The cross on which Jesus died was placed on Golgotha's hill just outside the gate of the city of Jerusalem. He suffered *outside the gate* that you and I, through faith in Him, might enter the gates of the Pearly White City.

7. *Everything was done by the priest.*

The leper did nothing except come to the priest,

state his need, and let the priest perform the ritual of cleansing. So it is with our cleansing from sin: *Jesus paid it all!*

"Not by works of righteousness *which WE have done,* but according to His mercy He saved us, by the washing of regeneration, and renewing of the Holy Ghost" (Tit. 3:5).

"For *by grace are ye saved through faith;* and that not of yourselves: it is the gift of God: not of works, lest any man should boast" (Eph. 2:8, 9).

"Yourself" and "works" are left out of it. A man is *"justified by FAITH* without the deeds of the law" (Rom. 3:28). *JESUS is our salvation.* He is the Door to heaven. He is the Way, the Truth, and the Life. No man can come to God but by His only begotten Son (John 14:6). "Neither is there salvation in any other: for there is none other name under heaven given among men, whereby we must be saved" (Acts 4:12).

Like the leper when he comes to the priest to make known his need, sinners come to Jesus—and He does the rest. When a person realizes that he is sin-sick, that he has a disease of the soul which only Jesus can cure, if he will come to Him in faith, believing that He is able, He will cleanse that one from all sin and write his name in the Lamb's book of life.

8. The bird must be killed *in an "earthen vessel."*

The earthen vessel represented the body of

Christ, a body of flesh. He was "made a little lower than the angels for the suffering of death, crowned with glory and honour; that He by the grace of God should taste death for every man" (Heb. 2:9).

"What the law could not do, in that it was weak through the flesh, God sending His own Son *in the likeness* of sinful flesh, and for sin, condemned sin in the flesh" (Rom. 8:3).

Jesus fulfilled every jot and tittle of God's holy law (Matt. 5:17, 18), and now—by the grace of God and through Christ's death on the cross—"we have this treasure in *earthen vessels*, that the excellency of the power may be of God, and not of us" (II Cor. 4:7). The earthen vessel used in cleansing the leper enables us to see (typically) the Lord Jesus being slain in His mortal body.

9. The bird was slain *by a direct command of God*.

It was also by the command of God that Jesus died for the sin of the world. He testified: "Therefore doth my Father love me, because I lay down my life, that I might take it again. No man taketh it from me, but I lay it down of myself. I have power to lay it down, and I have power to take it again. *This COMMANDMENT have I received of my Father*" (John 10:17, 18).

It was not merely a *suggestion* that Jesus die for the sin of the world. It was in accordance with

God's will and by His command that Jesus went to the cross and suffered an ignominious death. Jesus "humbled Himself, and became *obedient unto DEATH, even the death of the cross*" (Phil. 2:8).

God "spared not His own Son, but delivered Him up for us all . . ." (Rom. 8:32). He "so loved the world, that He gave His only begotten Son, that whosoever believeth in Him should not perish, but have everlasting life" (John 3:16). God "sent His Son to be the propitiation for our sins" (I John 4:10). Therefore "*we also JOY IN GOD* through our Lord Jesus Christ, by whom we have now received the atonement" (Rom. 5:11). We rejoice in the Lord Jesus for His dying on the cross, but we also joy in God the Father because He was willing to *send* His only begotten Son to die on the cross for wicked sinners such as you and I.

10. The bird must be killed *over running water.*

In the Bible, *water* is a symbol of the Word of God. In John 15:3 Jesus said to His disciples, "Now ye are *clean* through *THE WORD which I have spoken unto you.*" The Apostle Paul tells us that Christ "loved the Church, and gave Himself for it; that He might *sanctify and cleanse it with the washing of water by THE WORD*" (Eph. 5:25, 26).

Running water symbolizes the Word and the Spirit in action:

"In the last day, that great day of the feast, Jesus stood and cried, saying: If any man thirst, let him come unto me, and drink. He that believeth on me, as the Scripture hath said, out of his belly shall flow rivers of *living water.* (*But this spake He of THE SPIRIT,* which they that believe on Him should receive: for the Holy Ghost was not yet given; because that Jesus was not yet glorified)" (John 7:37-39).

From these passages of Holy Writ we can clearly see that *water* in the Bible is a symbol of the Word of God being made *alive and active* by the operation of the Holy Spirit—"Except a man be born *of water* (the Word) and *the Spirit,* he cannot enter into the kingdom of God" (John 3:5).

11. The *live* bird was *dipped in the blood* of the bird that had been killed.

Thus, the living bird was identified with the bird which had been slain, and bore the marks and stains of that sacrifice. The Word of God presents no more beautiful picture of the resurrection of the Lord Jesus Christ!

The risen Lord bears the marks of the cross. When He appeared to His disciples after His resurrection, "they were terrified and affrighted, and supposed that they had seen a spirit." They thought they were seeing only the spirit or ghost of Jesus. But "He said unto them, . . . *Behold my hands and my feet,* that it is I myself. Handle me, and see; for a spirit hath not flesh and bones, as ye see me have. *And when He had thus spoken, HE SHEWED THEM HIS HANDS AND HIS FEET"* (Luke 24:36-40).

It was by the marks of the cross—the scars in His hands, His feet, and His side—that Thomas laid aside his doubt and acknowledged the risen Christ. Thomas had said to the other disciples, "Except I shall see in His hands *the print of the nails,* and put my finger into the print of the nails, and *thrust my hand into His side, I will not believe!"* But when Jesus appeared the second time to the disciples when Thomas was present, He invited the skeptical disciple, "Reach hither thy finger, and behold my hands; and reach hither thy hand, and thrust it into my side." Thomas at once exclaimed, *"My Lord and my God!"* (John 20:24-28).

It is by the marks of the cross that the nation Israel will recognize their Messiah when He comes to earth again: "And one shall say unto Him, *What are these wounds IN THINE HANDS?* Then He shall answer, Those with which I was wounded in the house of my friends" (Zech. 13:6).

Many times during my ministry I have been asked, "Will Jesus have the scars of the nails in His hands and feet? and will He have the scar in His pierced side, and the scars of the thorn-crown on His brow?" My reply is always, *"Yes."* I believe the Word of God teaches that Jesus will still wear the scars which were put there by sin, and I believe the scars will make us love Him more. They will deepen our appreciation for the suffering He endured and the sacrifice He made for us!

12. The living bird was then *released*.

Christ died *once,* for *all.* His one offering was perfect. Therefore in resurrection He is forevermore freed from death and judgment. In His sacrificial death He *conquered* death, hell, and the grave, and He lives to die no more! *"Christ being raised from the dead DIETH NO MORE. Death hath no more dominion over Him"* (Rom. 6:9).

Thus do we *who believe on Jesus* have everlasting life. *WE live because HE lives and His immortality is imparted to us.* If He delays His coming for the Church, we will die in the flesh. We are born of parents who die, but in the spiritual life we will live eternally because we are born of an Eternal Father.

13. The living bird *rose up into the air.*

Released, free to soar on high, the living bird ascending into the sky is silent but eloquent witness that the risen Christ would also ascend as the living and immortal Man, to take His place at the right hand of God. "For there is one God, and *one Mediator between God and men—THE*

MAN CHRIST JESUS" (I Tim. 2:5).

After His resurrection, Jesus "shewed Himself alive . . . by many infallible proofs, being seen of (the apostles) forty days, and speaking of the things pertaining to the kingdom of God" (Acts 1:3). He was seen "of the twelve," and on one occasion He was seen of "above five hundred brethren at once." He was seen of Peter, of James, and of all the apostles (I Cor. 15:5-7).

Then when His time on earth was accomplished, He led the disciples "out as far as to Bethany, and He lifted up His hands, and blessed them. And it came to pass, while He blessed them, He was parted from them, and carried up into heaven" (Luke 24:50, 51).

When Jesus ascended into heaven and sat down at the right hand of God, He took with Him the blood of His own sacrifice as a precious and eternal memorial. What an offering He made to the Father in our behalf! *". . . BY HIS OWN BLOOD He entered in once into the holy place, having obtained eternal redemption for us"* (Heb. 9:12).

14. The leper who desired to be cleansed must come *to the priest*.

Just as the leper had to come to the priest and confess his need for cleansing, so Jesus continually invites men to come to Him for cleansing from sin:

"Come unto me, all ye that labour and are

heavy laden . . ." (Matt. 11:28).

"Come unto me, and drink" (John 7:37b).

"Him that cometh to me *I will in no wise cast out"* (John 6:37).

15. The leper was to be sprinkled *"seven times."*

Seven is God's number for perfection. *Naaman* was told to wash seven times in the river Jordan to be cleansed from *his* leprosy. (Read II Kings 5:10-14.) The leper who came to the priest for cleansing was to be sprinkled seven times with the blood of the dead bird, but when our Great High Priest, the Lord Jesus Christ, applies His blood to our sinful souls, the cleansing is *perfect and complete.* "The blood of Jesus Christ . . . cleanseth us *from ALL sin"* (I John 1:7b). John the Beloved proclaims "glory and dominion for ever and ever" (Rev. 1:6) *"unto Him that loved us, and WASHED US FROM OUR SINS IN HIS OWN BLOOD"* (Rev. 1:5).

Our Great High Priest is willing and anxious to *apply the blood*, but only in answer to our faith. We must *believe His Word*, for the cleansing blood is applied only by faith. Jesus confessed that He "did not many mighty works" in His own community because of the unbelief of the people there (Matt. 13:57, 58). *UNBELIEF renders Him powerless.* He can cleanse from sin only if we *believe*, for *it is FAITH that brings the cleansing blood to the needy heart.*

16. The cleansed leper *had a living witness.*

For proof that he was clean in God's sight, the cleansed leper could point to the living bird, circling in the heavens above him, bearing the marks and stains of the blood of the bird that had been slain.

How can I be certain that I am saved, cleansed from sin and made ready for heaven? Because "my Witness (Jesus) is in heaven, and my record is on high!" (Job 16:19). Therefore I can say with Paul, "Who is he that condemneth? *It is CHRIST that died, yea rather, that is risen again, who is even at the right hand of God, who also maketh intercession for us"* (Rom. 8:34).

I am so glad that one day I received the blood of Jesus for the remission of my sins. I am glad He lives to confess me before my heavenly Father. I am so thankful that He has my record, that I know Him as my personal Saviour, and that I have the witness of the Spirit in my heart—for "the Spirit Himself beareth witness with our spirit, that we are the children of God" (Rom. 8:16).

Dear reader, have YOU been cleansed from sin? If not, then please believe on the Lord Jesus Christ and be saved (Acts 16:31).

Receive Jesus' blood and be cleansed (I John 1:7).

The risen Lord, our Great High Priest, is even now seated at the right hand of the Father, anxiously awaiting your coming to Him for cleansing.

Remember: *God is "not willing that ANY should perish, but that ALL should come to repentance"* (II Pet. 3:9).

If you will come to Jesus, confessing your sins, and ask Him to save you and cleanse you with His precious blood, He will do it—and you will know it because He will give you the witness of the Spirit in your heart.

THE THREEFOLD PARABLE

The Threefold Parable

Our study in this message will be taken from the fifteenth chapter of the Gospel of Luke, verses 3 through 24. Many Bible teachers speak of this passage as containing three different parables which were spoken by our Lord, but there is actually but *ONE parable* in the chapter. Verse 3 tells us, "He (Jesus) spake *this parable* unto them." So there is *one parable* in *three parts,* and in those three parts we see the work of the entire Godhead in saving a sinner. God the Father, God the Son, and God the Holy Spirit all have a part in salvation. *God the Son* came into the world to seek and to save the lost. In this Day of Grace, *the Holy Spirit,* through the Church, is seeking the sinner. *God the Father* with exceeding joy receives the sinner who turns to Him, welcoming that sinner into the family of heaven as a son to all the provisions of God's love.

Also in this parable we see the sinner in three categories:

We see him as *a wanderer*—the lost sheep.
We see him as *a lost value*—the lost coin.
We see him as *a squanderer*—the lost son.

149

By Grace

The Lost Sheep

"He spake this parable unto them, saying:
What man of you, having an hundred sheep, if
he lose one of them, doth not leave the ninety
and nine in the wilderness (or pasture), and go
after that which is lost, until he find it? And
when he hath found it, he layeth it on his shoulders, rejoicing. And when he cometh home, he
calleth together his friends and neighbours, saying
unto them, Rejoice with me; for I have found my
sheep which was lost. *I say unto you, that likewise joy shall be in heaven over one sinner that
repenteth, more than over ninety and nine just
persons, which need no repentance*" (Luke 15:3-7).

We must keep in mind the fact that this is a
parable. In applying its meaning it is important
that the one great lesson of salvation be kept in
view, without pressing every little detail too far
in an effort to find a spiritual meaning for every
word, comma, and period. To do this would be
to find ourselves in great difficulty. As an old
adage expresses it, "If you squeeze a parable too
far you will draw blood, not milk, from it."

The first part of our parable presents a perfect
picture of the Good Shepherd (the Lord Jesus
Christ) who "giveth His life for the sheep" (John
10:11). You will notice that the sheep *left* the fold
of its own accord, the shepherd did not drive it
away. This is true of the sinner. The Lord Jesus
Christ invites and receives sinners, He does not

drive them away—or as He Himself expressed it, "Him that cometh to me I will in no wise cast out" (John 6:37).

The shepherd knew that one of his sheep was missing—lost in the mountains among deep ravines and barren hills, with danger all around and ravenous wolves seeking its life. And what did the shepherd do? He left the remainder of his flock—the ninety-and-nine that had not gone astray; he left the warmth and safety of the sheepfold; and he set out alone in search of the one lost sheep. He wasted no time complaining that the road was too rough and the hills too steep. He did not grumble and complain that the sheep had no business straying away in the first place. He simply went out to search—and please note that he did not search for a time and then give up! Oh, no! He searched *until he FOUND the sheep that was lost.* Then he lifted it gently in his arms, placed it on his shoulders, and carried it back to the fold.

When the shepherd arrived home he called his friends and neighbors together and said, "Rejoice with me! for I have found my sheep which was lost." If we had time and space here to take a brief journey into historical Palestine and the customs of that country, we would understand that the loss of a sheep was of much more concern to the oriental shepherd of the days when Jesus walked on earth than it is in our western world where sheep ranching is more or less an impersonal business. The eastern shepherd knew his sheep and the sheep knew his voice. Thus when he gave his own familiar call they followed him. It was a matter of personal pride and responsibility that the shepherd lose none of his flock. He protected them from wolves, from other dangers that threatened, and if need be he even *gave his life* in the interest of guarding his flock. This is all explained in John chapter 10 where Jesus gave His discourse on the Good Shepherd. Therefore when the Palestinian shepherd searched for a lost sheep, found it, and brought it back to the fold, it was an occasion for other shepherds and friends to rejoice with him.

That is why those to whom Jesus gave the parable of the Good Shepherd understood so well what He meant when He said, "Likewise joy shall be in heaven over one sinner that repenteth, more than over ninety and nine just persons, which need no repentance."

To understand God's love in the least we must realize that our Good Shepherd, the Lord Jesus Christ, knew mankind was lost. Every sinner is a wanderer—wandering away from God in every respect. In the unregenerate man, the mind, the nature, every intent of the heart, is evil until that lost soul is found by the Good Shepherd. It was for the sake of poor lost sinners that the Lord Jesus Christ left the heavenly creatures of righteousness who need no repentance and traveled all the way from heaven's glory to this wilderness of sin *to seek and to save "that which was lost"* (Luke 19:10). God the Son left His home in heaven, took upon Himself the form of man, and came into this world to lay His life down for those who are lost, wandering away from God.

I want you to see this picture, beloved: Just as the shepherd in the parable lifted the lost sheep in his arms, put it across his shoulders and carried it back to the fold, just so does our Good Shepherd put His mighty arms underneath and around us, and in His great love and omnipotence He will bear us all the way to the gate of the Heavenly Fold! He came to seek me, He came to seek you. It is not His will that any should perish, but that all should come to repentance (II Pet. 3:9). He is seeking every sinner no matter how far in sin that one has wandered. *Have YOU answered His call?*

The Lost Coin

"What woman having ten pieces of silver, if she lose one piece, doth not light a candle, and sweep the house, and seek diligently till she find it? And when she hath found it, she calleth her friends and her neighbours together, saying, Rejoice with me; for I have found the piece which I had lost. Likewise, I say unto you, there is joy in the presence of the angels of God over one sinner that repenteth" (Luke 15:8-10).

In the preaching and teaching of Jesus, He used illustrations from familiar things, things that were easily understood by His hearers. It was customary for women in that land to carry money on their headbands. They put tiny holes in silver or gold coins and fastened them to the band which they were accustomed to wear about their head. I have seen women in Judaea with eight or ten pieces of silver fastened to the band across their foreheads. Such was the case of the woman in this parable. She had ten pieces of money, and she lost one of them.

This coin had the king's image stamped upon it; and since the coin was lost, the king's image was also lost, the money was out of circulation and doing no one any good. It was no longer of value to the woman to whom it belonged, it was of no value to the king or to the state.

Like the lost coin, man without God is lost from his rightful owner, he is in darkness. Man is created in the image of God (Gen. 1:26, 27), but the sinner does not show forth the *likeness* of God in his life. The image of the Creator is hidden, and like the lost coin the sinner is of no value to himself, no value to God, and there is no reason at all why he should exist!

But a human soul is very valuable to the Lord Jesus Christ. Heaven's most precious Jewel was the price required to redeem the lost soul of man.

Jesus Himself valued a soul more than the riches of the entire world. He asked, "What is a man profited, if he shall gain the whole world, and lose his own soul? or what shall a man give in exchange for his soul?" (Matt. 16:26).

"The carnal mind (the mind we have through the fall of man) is enmity against God: for it is not subject to the law of God, neither indeed can be. . . . The natural man receiveth not the things of the Spirit of God: for they are foolishness unto him: neither can he know them, because they are spiritually discerned" (Rom. 8:7; I Cor. 2:14). Man's moral and spiritual ruin in his separation from God is most tragic! The person who does not know "the Light of the world" is indeed groping in sad spiritual darkness!

Now the woman in this second part of our parable is a symbol of the Church. The Bible declares the Church to be *"a chaste virgin" espoused to Christ,* and Revelation 19:7 says, "Let us be glad and rejoice, and give honour to Him: for *the marriage of the Lamb is come, and His wife hath made herself ready."* As the woman in the parable is diligently seeking for the lost coin, so the business of the Church is to seek lost souls—lost men and women who are intended to bear the image of God.

The business of the Church is not to entertain the world, reform the world, or improve world conditions. The Church is to be a soul-winning business. (Please notice I did not say "a membership-driving business," but the business of winning souls, leading people to Jesus.) The woman in the parable did not say, "O, well! There is no need to spend time *searching* for the coin. I am sure it will come to light sooner or later." No, she searched until she *found* the coin! The Church has the message with which to find souls—if we would only use that message.

We notice that the woman in the parable had a *"candle"*—literally, *a lamp,* and we know what the lamp represents: *"THY WORD is a lamp unto my feet, and a light unto my path"* (Psalm 119:105). God highly honored the Church when He bestowed upon that body the right to possess and give forth His Words of life, and the Church should never speak without backing up what is said with *"Thus saith the LORD."* The "lamp" is the Word of God and the "light" is the truth the Word gives forth. We must remember that the Bible does not simply *"contain"* the Word of God, *the Bible IS the Word of God, penned by "holy men of God . . . as they were moved by the Holy Ghost"* (II Pet. 1:21).

The woman in the parable also had a *broom,* for we are told that she *swept the house,* seeking diligently, until she found the coin. The broom symbolizes the energy and power of the Church— "Not by might, nor by power, *but by my Spirit,* saith the Lord of hosts" (Zech. 4:6). The success of the Church does not depend upon an educated ministry, trained workers, a large and well-filled treasury, or influential members. The Church is empowered by the Holy Spirit, and the local church that does not depend on the Holy Spirit for power and success is a total failure.

This is clearly seen in the church at Laodicea— a church that was rich, increased with goods, in need of nothing, materially speaking. But what did the Lord say of that church? He said, "I know thy works, that thou art neither cold nor hot: I would thou wert cold or hot. So then because thou art lukewarm, and neither cold nor hot, *I will spue thee out of my mouth!* Because thou sayest, I am rich, and increased with goods, and have need of nothing; *and knowest not that thou art wretched, and miserable, and poor, and blind, and naked"* (Rev. 3:15-17). The lukewarm church, needing nothing materially but lacking the power of the Spirit, made God sick—*spewed* out instead of being *caught* out as the true Church will be at the Rapture.

The Lost Son

"A certain man had two sons: and the younger of them said to his father, Father, give me the portion of goods that falleth to me. And he divided unto them his living. And not many days after the younger son gathered all together, and took his journey into a far country, and there wasted his substance with riotous living.

"And when he had spent all, there arose a mighty famine in that land; and he began to be in want. And he went and joined himself to a citizen of that country; and he sent him into his fields to feed swine. And he would fain have filled his belly with the husks that the swine did eat: and no man gave unto him.

"And when he came to himself, he said, How many hired servants of my father's have bread enough and to spare, and I perish with hunger! I will arise and go to my father, and will say unto him, Father, I have sinned against heaven, and before thee, and am no more worthy to be called thy son: make me as one of thy hired servants.

"And he arose, and came to his father. But when he was yet a great way off, his father saw him, and had compassion, and ran, and fell on his neck, and kissed him. And the son said unto him, Father, I have sinned against heaven, and in thy sight, and am no more worthy to be called thy son. But the father said to his servants, Bring forth the best robe, and put it on him; and put a ring on his hand, and shoes on his feet: and bring hither the fatted calf, and kill it; and let us eat, and be merry: for this my son was dead, and is alive again; he was lost, and is found. And they began to be merry" (Luke 15:11-24).

Like the wayward son in our parable, the sinner

is a *squanderer*. He squanders life, health, strength, time, and opportunity. He squanders the chance to know God, possess peace, have a home in heaven, and enjoy eternal life instead of suffering eternal death in the lake of fire after this life is over. In this part of the parable we clearly see the *logic* of sin and the *suicidal outcome* of sin.

Notice that this younger son wanted what was coming to him—and he got it. In other words, he wanted his inheritance in *this* life. Christians are pilgrims and strangers on earth. We have no certain dwellingplace (I Cor. 4:11). Our citizenship is in heaven (Phil. 3:20), and we look "for a city which hath foundations, whose builder and maker is God" (Heb. 11:10). The Christian's inheritance comes later—"an inheritance incorruptible, and undefiled, and that fadeth not away, *reserved in heaven" for us* (I Pet. 1:4). Meanwhile, in this life Jesus invites, *"If any man will come after me, let him DENY HIMSELF, and take up his CROSS, and follow me"* (Matt. 16:24).

He also said, "He that loveth father or mother more than me is not worthy of me: and he that loveth son or daughter more than me is not worthy of me. *And he that taketh not his CROSS, and followeth after me, is not worthy of me"* (Matt. 10:37, 38). In Luke 14:27 He declared, *"Whosoever doth NOT bear his cross, and come after me, cannot be my disciple!"*

But then Jesus promises, "Every one that hath forsaken houses, or brethren, or sisters, or father, or mother, or wife, or children, or lands, for my name's sake, shall receive *an hundredfold,* and shall inherit *everlasting life*" (Matt. 19:29). Romans 8:17 tells us that we are heirs of God, joint-heirs with Christ, and that if we suffer with Him we will also be glorified with Him. In II Timothy 2:12 we read, "If we suffer, we shall also reign with Him. If we deny Him, He also will deny us."

So the Christian's inheritance is yet to come. In other words, Jesus said, "Follow me—and I will put a cross on your back. Follow me—and we will walk together under the yoke. *Suffer* with me—and we will reign together. Deny yourself houses and lands, loved ones and friends in order to follow me, and you will be restored an hundredfold in the world to come!" But the young man in our parable wanted his inheritance in this life, and having obtained that inheritance he took his journey into a far country and wasted his substance in riotous living.

When any person—young or old—takes a journey without the guiding hand of the Good Shepherd, every day traveled is a day wasted; and the road traveled without the leadership of the Holy Spirit will lead to the land of *eternal waste.* Proverbs 3:6 admonishes us, "In all thy ways acknowledge Him, and He shall direct thy paths"—and you may be sure that those paths will not lead to the pigpen, as did the path of this wayward son!

"And when he had spent all, there arose *a mighty famine* in that land; and he began to be *in want.*" Such is the perpetual state of the sinner! Money will not buy that which satisfies the soul; and while this boy was no doubt in *physical* want, he was also in *spiritual* want. His *soul* was in the midst of famine. Isaiah 55:2 asks, "Wherefore do ye spend money for that which is not bread? and your labour for that which satisfieth not? Hearken diligently unto me, and eat ye that which is good, and let your soul delight itself in fatness!"

The young man in our parable finally became so destitute that he "joined himself to a citizen of that country; and he sent him into his fields to feed *swine.*" Lo, how the mighty have fallen! This son of a wealthy, noble father, hiring himself out as a day laborer—not to do farm work, not to watch after sheep and cattle, but *to tend pigs!* The sinner who labors to feed the lusts of the flesh will eventually find himself in *spiritual degradation* equal to the position this young man occupied as a feeder of swine. To the Jew, nothing could be lower, nothing could be more contaminating and degrading.

Not only did the boy find it necessary to do this humiliating work in order to earn enough to keep body and soul together, he also reached a state of hunger that made him want to *eat* with the hogs—*"and NO MAN gave unto him!"* How typical of the sinner this is, for the person lost and steeped in sin can find no relief in his fellow-man. His help must come from God, from the heavenly Father, just as this boy obtained no help until he "came to himself" and decided to return to his father.

Yes, *"when he came to himself"*—i. e., one day he became painfully aware of the contrast in his present position and the place he had occupied as the beloved son of a provident father! I can well imagine that he looked at the ragged, filthy rags he was wearing—rags and tatters that had once been the elaborate raiment to which a rich man's son was accustomed. He looked at his feet, bare now except for the mud and filth of the hogpen.

This had no doubt been a proud young man when things were going his way. As long as his money held out he had an abundance of friends, and his social life had been among the elite. But as he thought of his father's house where even the servants were richly fed, and as he contemplated the sad condition in which he now found himself, pride was no more! Gladly would he take his place as a *servant* in his father's house, considering himself no longer worthy to be called a son.

Here again we see the typical characteristics

of the sinner. God cannot do business with a proud person. The sinner must come to the place where he *sees* himself *as* a sinner in need of a Saviour, *deserving* nothing better than condemnation but asking a loving Father for forgiveness and willing to do whatever God asks him to do. When he reaches that place, he is in a position to do business with God.

This young man reached a decision—and acted upon it. He immediately started for the father's house. We are not told how long a journey lay before him, but one thing is certain! The father had been looking for the son's return, for verse 20 tells us, "When he was yet a great way off, his father saw him, and had compassion, and ran, and fell on his neck, and kissed him!" I do not doubt that the father in our parable had been looking in the direction of that lost boy ever since the boy left home, and the minute he reached the brow of the last hill the father recognized him. He did not wait to hear the son's confession and request for forgiveness. He ran to meet him, embraced him, and kissed him.

Our heavenly Father commended His love toward us, "in that, *while we were yet sinners, Christ died for us*" (Rom. 5:8). Think of it, beloved: When we were very, very unlovely, Jesus loved us enough to come into this world and die for us. He saw us, you and me, even the day He died on the cross for our sins! Yes, God the

Father saw us a long time ago, hogpen clothes and all—and made provision for our salvation. He is always ready to kiss away the guilt and shame of a poor sinner who comes home.

Sitting by the pigpen the boy had decided what he would say to his father. He would confess, "Father, I have sinned against heaven, and before thee, and am no more worthy to be called thy son: make me as one of thy hired servants." The warm welcome he received from his father did not change his story one bit. He began his confession. He said, "Father, I have sinned against heaven, and in thy sight, and am no more worthy to be called thy son"—and that is as far as he got! He had confessed that he had sinned, and that was enough. The father did not let him finish. Joyfully he cried out, "Bring forth the best robe, and put it on him; and put a ring on his hand, and shoes on his feet: and bring hither the fatted calf, and kill it; and let us eat, and be merry: *for this MY SON was dead, and is alive again;* he was lost, and is found!"

Sinners who confess their sins are not made servants. *They become SONS:*

"When the fulness of the time was come, God sent forth His Son, made of a woman, made under the law, to redeem them that were under the law, that we might receive the adoption of sons. And because ye are sons, God hath sent forth the Spirit of His Son into your hearts, crying,

Abba, Father. Wherefore thou art no more a servant, but a son; and if a son, then an heir of God through Christ" (Gal. 4:4-7).

The prodigal son, now feasting at his father's table, had asked and received his inheritance, and he had spent every penny of it in riotous living. He had wilfully wasted his part of his father's estate—and now he sits at his father's table feasting on the father's bountiful supply of provisions. *Beloved, that is GRACE!* pure, unearned, unmerited *favor!* The father could have made the boy a slave and forced him to work hard for every morsel of bread he ate from that table—and justly so. Or he could justifiably have sent the boy away. Those would have been the just deserts of such a prodigal—but the father had compassion on him, welcomed him home, and gave him a son's place at the table.

Just so, God could have annihilated Adam and Eve when they sinned in the Garden of Eden. He could have destroyed the entire human race— and He would have been justified in so doing. But His great grace prompted so great a love for mankind, that He provided a covering for the nakedness of Adam and Eve, and fashioned the plan of salvation—a plan carried out and paid for with the shed blood of His only begotten Son— that you and I might receive forgiveness for sins and be made sons of God and joint-heirs with Christ to the joys and glories of heaven! *GRACE, all of grace, nothing merited, deserved, or earned on our part!*

Yes, this threefold parable presents a perfect picture of the sinner and of God's loving provision for salvation. A sheep is definitely out of place anywhere but in the sheepfold, and when the shepherd found that one sheep was missing he forgot all else—he forgot his needed rest, he forgot the darkness of the night and the danger of the journey he must make in his search for his sheep. The all-important thing to him was that one of his flock had wandered into the desert, alone and in danger, and he sought until he found the sheep and returned it to the fold.

Thus did Jesus, our Good Shepherd, come into this wilderness of sin, and He stayed here until He fulfilled every demand of the heavenly Father, thereby making it possible for sinners to be found and brought into the fold of God.

The coin, lost in the darkness of an unswept house, was of no value to anyone as long as it remained lost. The same is true of the sinner. The soul of man is worth more than all the silver and gold in all the world, but a *lost soul* is of no value to anyone. God cannot use it as long as it is lost. It cannot show forth the image of the Creator as long as it is lost. But when that soul is saved, the Holy Spirit dwells within; and by our good deeds the men and women around us see Jesus reflected in our lives.

The prodigal son is certainly typical of the sinner. Every sinner is a squanderer, a wastrel. Every good and perfect gift comes from God (James 1:17)—even the air we breathe and the sunshine and rain that cause life to continue on this planet. When men live for self, serving divers lusts and pleasures, they are squandering and wasting what has been bestowed upon them by another. Every moment lived for the devil is wasted. Everything done in the energy of the flesh is wasted. But thank God, when sinners "come to themselves" and see their need of a Saviour, when they humble themselves and confess their sins, God saves them for Jesus' sake and makes them sons, with all the joy and privileges of sonship!

Moreover, the saving of a sinner starts a praise service in Paradise! "Joy shall be in heaven over one sinner that repenteth. . . . There is joy in the presence of the angels of God over one sinner that repenteth."

Someone may be asking, "How do you really *get saved?*" You do exactly as the prodigal did— he realized that he was in the wrong place, he was disgusted with his condition, and he determined to do something about it. So he returned to his father's house, confessed that he had sinned, and the father forgave him and prepared a feast to welcome him home. So far as Scripture records, the father *completely forgot* the "far country" episode.

167

So, unsaved friend, if you see yourself as a sinner, if you are sick of the sinful life you are living and you want your life from now on to count for Christ, just confess your sins to the heavenly Father, ask Him to forgive you and save you for Jesus' sake—and He will do it! Not only will He save you, but He will cast your sins behind His back and remember them no more (Isa. 38:17; Heb. 8:12). He will cast your sins into the depths of the sea (Mic. 7:19). "For as the heaven is high above the earth, so great is His mercy toward them that fear Him. As far as the east is from the west, *SO FAR hath He removed our transgressions from us*" (Psalm 103: 11, 12).

To be justified by the blood of Jesus is to be just as though you had never sinned. The blood of Jesus cleanses *from ALL sin* (I John 1:7) and when God looks at the born again believer He sees only the perfection of His only begotten Son. Thus He forgives us for Jesus' sake and we are "accepted IN THE BELOVED" (Eph. 1:6).

**NO BARRIERS – NO LIMITATIONS –
NO SECRETS – NO OBSTACLES**

No Barriers — No Limitations —
No Secrets — No Obstacles

The fourth chapter of the Gospel of John will
furnish the text for our study in this message.
This passage of Scripture plainly teaches that
the love of God knows no limitations and recog-
nizes no obstacles. It sweeps away all barriers
that divide mankind.   When one is born into
the family of God by faith, baptized into the body
of Christ by the Holy Spirit and made partaker
of divine nature through the miracle of God, all
barriers—racial, social, or religious—fade away and
we become one in Christ, members of His body,
bone of His bone and flesh of His flesh (Eph.
5:30).   In the New Testament Church, the body
of Christ, "there is neither Greek nor Jew, cir-
cumcision nor uncircumcision, Barbarian, Scythian,
bond nor free: but Christ is all, and in all"
(Col. 3:11).

No Barriers

"When therefore the Lord knew how the Pharisees had heard that Jesus made and baptized
more disciples than John, (though Jesus Himself
baptized not, but His disciples,) He left Judaea,

and departed again into Galilee. And He must needs go through Samaria. Then cometh He to a city of Samaria, which is called Sychar, near to the parcel of ground that Jacob gave to his son Joseph.

"Now Jacob's well was there. Jesus therefore, being wearied with His journey, sat thus on the well: and it was about the sixth hour. There cometh a woman of Samaria to draw water. Jesus saith unto her, *Give me to drink.* (For His disciples were gone away unto the city to buy meat.) Then saith the woman of Samaria unto Him, *How is it that thou, being a Jew, askest drink of me, which am a woman of Samaria?* for the Jews have no dealings with the Samaritans. Jesus answered and said unto her, If thou knewest the gift of God, and who it is that saith to thee, Give me to drink, thou wouldest have asked of Him, *and He would have given thee living water"* (John 4:1-10).

"He MUST needs go through Samaria." Every step Jesus took on this earth and every word He spoke was by divine counsel and appointment. His every act was in fulfillment of His mission here, and of His determination to do the Father's will. His need to go through Samaria and His visit to Jacob's well did not come about by accident. They were foreordained before the foundation of the world.

Jesus was God in flesh, therefore He was omniscient. He knew what was in the mind of man, He knew the history of mankind—past, present, and future. He knew all things. Therefore His need to go through Samaria on His journey from Judaea to Galilee was because there was a thirsty soul waiting to drink of the water of life. The chances are that she would never have come to Him, so He went where she was and carried the message of life to her.

When Jesus and His disciples reached Jacob's well near the city of Sychar, He *"being wearied with His journey"* sat down on the well to rest while His disciples went on into the city to buy food. I appreciate the statement in this verse so very much because it proves the reality of the humanity of Jesus! Very God in flesh, yet very man; possessing the divine attributes of God, yet in His humanity becoming weary, thirsty, hungry— just as you and I, except that He was sinless. Here we see His infinite compassion, His humility and condescension. He who made the world and all that therein is, to whom the cattle on a thousand hills belong, was content to take a body of flesh and come to earth to walk the dusty roads of Judaea and Galilee to seek and to save the lost. There is no place in the Holy Scriptures where we are told that Jesus ever rode in a carriage or on horseback as a king might travel in those days. The only record given of His riding was when He rode into Jerusalem on a donkey in fulfillment of prophecy of the Old Testament.

Thus, like any other man who was tired, He sat down on the stones that were built up around Jacob's well. *"And it was about the sixth hour."* According to the time used in those days, this would have been about twelve o'clock—high noon —the hottest, sultriest time of the day. No doubt the sun was shining full strength, with not even the faintest breeze to refresh the face of Jesus as He sat on the well to rest.

"There cometh a woman of Samaria to draw water." It was customary in that country for the women to draw water for use in the home. This is still true to a great extent. Not too many years ago I visited that area, and I made some beautiful color movies of the women coming to the wells at daybreak to draw water. But we notice two unusual things about this woman of Samaria: First of all, it was customary for the women to come to the wells in early morning, even at dawn, to draw water for the day. Secondly, they came in groups, not singly. The fact that this woman came alone indicated that she had no friends among the women of the community—and this is understandable from the standpoint of her character. As we will learn a bit later, she was a woman of *questionable* character, a home-wrecker, more associated with the men of her acquaintance than with the ladies. That she came at *noon* indicates that she did not care

to encounter other women at the well, for no doubt they treated her with scorn and contempt.

As she approached the well on this particular day she saw a stranger awaiting her. He was easily recognizable as a Jew, and that fact was, in itself, of interest to her, for the Jews did not pass through Samaria if they could possibly avoid it. We will discuss this more fully a bit later in our study.

Jesus knew all about this woman, but even so, He did not open the conversation by rebuking her because of her ungodly living. Instead He asked a favor of her. He said, *"Give me to drink."* She answered Him with a question: "How is it that thou, *being a JEW*, askest drink of *me,* which am a woman of *Samaria?"* The woman was understandably surprised. Historians tell us that the Jews usually traveled through Peraea, across the Jordan, on their way from Judaea to Galilee, in order to avoid going through Samaria. It was a longer route, but so great was the hatred of the Jews for the Samaritans that they preferred the inconvenience of the longer route to traveling *through* that country!

But Jesus was a different kind of Jew. He had no hatred, no prejudice or animosity, toward any man. He came into the world to seek and to save the lost—whosoever would believe on His finished work. It is true that He came first to the Jews, and in the early part of His ministry

He instructed His disciples to go to the lost sheep of the house of Israel; but even in this journey through Samaria He was teaching them that God's saving grace is for "whosoever will."

You will notice Jesus did not answer the woman's question. He knew that this was not the time to discuss the conditions that existed between the Jews and the Samaritans. He knew this poor, sinful woman was but one step from hell, and He loved her soul—steeped though it was in the scarlet sin of adultery. He knew that her curiosity and interest had been aroused, and when He spoke again it was to lead her another step toward the gift of God, the gift of His saving grace, and the water of life:

"If thou knewest the gift of God and who it is that saith to thee, Give me to drink, thou wouldest have asked of Him, and *He would have given thee living water.*" Jesus could have said to this woman, "If you knew who I am, you would ask of me and I would have mercy on your poor, adulterous life and save you by grace." But at this stage of the conversation if He had mentioned *grace, mercy,* and *the new birth* she would not have known what He was talking about because she was spiritually ignorant. She had not received the light of the Word of God, and she would have turned away from Him. But He spoke to her of *living water.* She had come to the well to draw water, and her curiosity was increased when He told her that he had water much better than the water she would draw from Jacob's well.

Living water for the asking! Certainly this brings out the point of this part of our study, that the love of God knows no racial or social barriers. Between this woman and the Lord Jesus Christ there were great barriers—*both racial and social.* No self-respecting Jew would have engaged in conversation with a Samaritan, and certainly not with a Samaritan of such ill repute as this woman. Socially there was an even *greater* barrier, for He was the Lamb of God, the Sinless One, upright as very God, while she was a social outcast whose soul was drenched in sin. But Jesus came not to be ministered unto, but to minister, and to give His life a ransom for just such poor, lost souls as this, and He always made a special effort to reach these outcasts of society, the downcast ones in the gutter. He never met a person so despicable that He could not reach out in love and compassion, to uplift, to heal, to offer God's gift of saving grace.

Sinner friend, it makes no difference to which religion or social class you belong—*Jesus loves you,* and if you will come to Him He will save you and make you a child of God. He loves all peoples—the white, the black, the rich, the poor, the wise, the unwise, the bond, the free— it is not His will that any should perish, but that all should come to repentance and be saved (II Pet. 3:9). I repeat—the love of God knows no racial or social barriers.

No Limitations

"The woman saith unto Him, Sir, thou hast nothing to draw with, and the well is deep. From whence then hast thou that living water? Art thou greater than our father Jacob, which gave us the well, and drank thereof himself, and his children, and his cattle?

"Jesus answered and said unto her, Whosoever drinketh of this water shall thirst again: but whosoever drinketh of the water that I shall give him shall never thirst; but the water that I shall give him shall be in him a well of water springing up into everlasting life" (John 4:11-14).

The provision of Almighty God knows no human limitations. The words Jesus spoke to this woman were the strangest words she had ever heard. Here sat a Man with no waterpots, no rope, no well bucket, no chain—*nothing* with which to draw water from a well that was deep. Yet with all calmness and confidence He had announced that He could furnish her with water that would quench her thirst forever! And the sincerity of His voice together with the look of compassion He gave her seemed to say, *"Believe it,* whether you *understand it* or not!"

God is not found by the wisdom of man. He

is not found by searching. He is not found under a microscope nor in a test tube. God is found by faith such as the faith of a little child. Jesus said, "Except ye be converted, and become *as little children*, ye shall not enter into the kingdom of heaven" (Matt. 18:3). We must take God at His Word—believe that He will do what He says He will do if we meet His conditions. God cannot lie (Heb. 6:18; Tit. 1:2), and His Word is forever settled in heaven (Psalm 119:89).

Notice the heavenly wisdom Jesus demonstrated in dealing with this Samaritan woman. She asked Him how He intended obtaining water from the well when He had nothing with which to draw it. "Art thou *greater than our father Jacob* who gave us this well?" Jesus could have started a first-rate religious argument here. He could easily—and truthfully—have said, "*Certainly* I am greater than Jacob!" He said to the doubting Pharisees, "*Before Abraham was, I AM!*" and He could have said the same to this woman, but He did not. Had He made such a statement to her He would have lost the opportunity to win her to salvation. He did not answer her question directly. He simply stated that those who drank of the water from Jacob's well would thirst again.

This was a fact the woman well knew, for she came day after day to draw water from the well to quench a thirst that returned again and again. The water of Jacob's well is specifically typical of temporal and material things. It was good water, just as there are many material things that are good; but material things do not satisfy the soul. Man is created in the image of Almighty God and he cannot be truly satisfied until his heart is right with God.

Jesus was God in flesh and the words He spoke were certainly the words of God. "Faith cometh by hearing, and hearing by the Word" (Rom. 10:17). As Jesus spoke to this woman about the living water, the Word began to create a thirst within her soul and she said, *"Sir, GIVE ME this water, that I thirst not, neither come hither to draw."*

No Secrets

"Jesus saith unto her, Go, call thy husband, and come hither. The woman answered and said, *I have no husband.* Jesus said unto her, *Thou hast well said, I have no husband: for thou hast had five husbands; and he whom thou now hast is not thy husband: in that saidst thou truly"* (John 4:16-18).

To God, there are no undiscovered, unknown secrets. He knows the innermost secrets of the heart (Psalm 44:21). The Psalmist declared, "Thou hast set our iniquities before thee, our secret sins in the light of thy countenance" (Psalm 90:8). Jesus Himself warned, "There is nothing covered that shall not be revealed; neither hid, that shall not be known. Therefore whatsoever ye have spoken in darkness shall be heard in the light; and that which ye have spoken in the ear in closets shall be proclaimed upon the housetops" (Luke 12:2, 3).

Jesus knew every secret of this woman's soul. He knew her great spiritual need, but He could not give her living water until she was willing to acknowledge that she was a sinner in need of a Saviour. Therefore He said to her, *"Go call thy husband,"* thus revealing to her that He knew the secrets of her soul, even the besetting sin that was robbing her of the peace and joy she longed for and which the "living water" would supply.

The woman replied, *"I have no husband."* It was at this point that Jesus clearly revealed His omniscience. He said, "Thou hast well said . . . for *thou hast had FIVE husbands*, and he whom thou now hast is *not* thy husband."

This Samaritan woman had been surprised that a Jew would condescend to speak to her. Now she was even *more* surprised, for she had not told this Man that she had had five husbands, she had not revealed her past life—and since He was a stranger in that city it was not likely that anyone else had told Him. Yet He very accurately described her life as it had been and as it was at that present time.

Not only did this unusual Person read the

history of her life to her, He refrained from any
ugly, ungracious comment on that life. He could
have said, "You are a wicked, adulterous woman
and unless you repent of your sins you will spend
eternity in hell!" But He said no word of re-
proach to her. Instead He commended her for
telling the truth. He said, "Thou hast well said
. . . in that saidst thou truly."

"The woman saith unto Him, *Sir, I perceive
that thou art a PROPHET*" (John 4:19). This
woman realized that she was dealing with a very
unusual Man. Gradually her poor, spiritually-
blinded eyes were opening. She had asked for
a drink of living water, but only faith can draw
living water from the well of God's salvation;
and while she had acknowledged Jesus as a *prophet* she had not yet recognized Him as *Messiah,
Saviour of mankind.*

Now notice how the devil attempted to side-
track the issue and get the woman's mind off
the subject of living water:

"Our fathers worshipped *in this mountain;* and
ye say, that *in Jerusalem* is the place where men
ought to worship. Jesus saith unto her, Woman,
believe me, the hour cometh, when ye shall neither
in this mountain, nor yet at Jerusalem, worship
the Father. Ye worship ye know not what: we
know what we worship: for salvation is of the
Jews. But the hour cometh, and now is, when
the true worshippers shall worship the Father

in spirit and in truth: for the Father seeketh such to worship Him. *God is a Spirit: and they that worship Him must worship Him in spirit and in truth"* (John 4:20-24).

The devil put into this woman's mind that she should ask Jesus—not about *salvation,* but where she should *worship.* He does the same thing today when he prompts sinners to ask—not "What must I do to be *saved?"* but *"Which church* do you think I should join?" You see, Satan cares not how "religious" you are nor how many churches you join just as long as you do not drink of the water of life. His aim is to keep you from embracing God's blood-bought salvation, and if he can keep you busy enough with outward religious activities and keep your mind occupied with things other than the salvation of your soul, he is perfectly happy about it! If Satan could have had this Samaritan woman to lead Jesus away from discussion of living water and into a discussion of the proper place to worship, there would have been no revival in Samaria. But this woman was not yet ready to worship. She was still unregenerated and it was only natural for her to think in terms of the religion of her fathers and follow the customs and traditions of the Samaritans, emphasizing the *place* of worship instead of the *Person* to whom worship was directed.

"The hour cometh...." Here the Lord is

declaring that a new dispensation was about to be ushered in—the Dispensation of the Gospel of Grace. There would be no more *distinction of places* such as the temple in Jerusalem or the mountain in Samaria. The "hour" was beginning at the very moment Jesus spoke those words, the hour when true worshippers would find the building or place of worship of little or no consequence. What counts in our worship is the internal state of the individual worshipper, the condition of the heart. Members of the Church of the living God do not worship according to the beauty of the building or its surroundings. They are concerned with the beauty of holiness which is found only in the finished work and shed blood of Jesus.

"God is a Spirit. . . . They that worship Him must worship Him *in spirit and in truth."* To worship "in spirit" means to worship from the heart, not in form, not carnal worship consisting of ceremonies, offerings, sacrifices, feasts, and keeping of days. Before Jesus shed His blood on Calvary, men worshipped through figures, types, and ceremonies; but when Jesus died, the veil was rent in twain and the holy of holies laid bare. Men then began to worship *in spirit*—and spirit is opposed to flesh. Believers today worship *"in truth"* as opposed to types and shadows. The sacrifices of the Mosaic system *pointed to the truth,* and *Jesus IS truth* (John 1:14; 14:6). He

was teaching this Samaritan woman that God is not like earthly kings, to be found in temples or in a mountain. God is the Eternal Spirit and He can accept only true worship—worship that proceeds from *a regenerated heart.*

The woman then said to Jesus, *"I know that Messias cometh, which is called Christ: when He is come, He will tell us all things"* (John 4:25). How did this sinful woman of Samaria know about the promised Messiah? The Scripture does not tell us, but our present verse clearly shows that at some time in her life she had been exposed to the teaching of the Old Testament prophecies. She not only knew Messiah would come, she also knew that when He came He would be able to discern *"all things."* This Man had told her things which, as mortal, He could not possibly have known because she had never seen Him before. He had first told her of "living water" and she had expressed a desire to *receive* the living water. He had then revealed her sin to her, and while He had ignored her question about the proper place to worship, He had clearly declared the necessity to worship God in spirit and in truth. She was now ready to receive a revelation concerning this Man with whom she was conversing.

No Obstacles

"Jesus saith unto her, *I THAT SPEAK UNTO*

THEE AM HE.... The woman then left her waterpot, and went her way into the city, and saith to the men, *Come, see a Man, which told me all things that ever I did. IS NOT THIS THE CHRIST?"* (John 4:26-29 in part).

This is posed as a question, but it is also a declaration. In other words, this woman testified, "This can be no other but the Christ, for only God's Messiah could do what this Man has just done!"

What brought this sinful soul to a knowledge of the Christ? The Word of God—*only seven words*—spoken by the Son of God, very God in flesh: *"I that speak unto thee am HE!"* The woman believed what Jesus said, and she was saved by God's grace when she exercised faith in His words.

What had Jesus told her about the "living water"? He had said, "The water that I shall give . . . shall be . . . *a well of water springing up into everlasting life!"* When salvation flooded the soul of this Samaritan woman she left her waterpot and ran into the city with an artesian well of living water bubbling in her own heart— and she gave the same invitation Jesus had given to the two disciples of John the Baptist: *"Come . . . see!"* (John 1:39). This was the same invitation Philip gave to Nathanael: *"Come . . . see!"* (John 1:46). We can give the same invitation today— "Come and see Jesus!"

Beloved, the power of the Word of God knows
no *insurmountable obstacles*. There is but one
Door to heaven, and that Door is opened by
grace through faith—faith in the finished work
and shed blood of the Lord Jesus Christ. *He
IS the Door to heaven* (John 10:9). It makes no
difference how far in sin one may go. It makes
no difference what color his skin may be, nor
what his nationality or social standing. It makes
no difference if he be millionaire or pauper, learned
or unlearned. All who would enter heaven must
enter by the Door, by faith in the finished plan
of salvation as set forth in the Word of God.

Therefore I declare that God's love knows no
racial or social barriers, it knows no human limitations. He sees every secret of the soul, and
His power knows no insurmountable obstacles.
Sinner friend, you have nothing hidden from God.
Your sins may be hidden from the eyes of your
friends and even from your family; but God sees
them, He knows all about them. And He is able
to do for you exactly what you need in your individual heart. If you will take Him at His
Word, bow your head before Him this moment
and believe in your heart that Jesus is the Christ,
Son of God, Saviour of the world, and accept
Him as your personal Saviour, He will save you—
and you will know it! And like this woman of
Samaria, you will have an artesian well of living
water bubbling in your soul, springing up into

everlasting life.

"Verily, verily, I say unto you, He that heareth my Word, and believeth on Him that sent me, *hath everlasting life, and shall not come into condemnation;* but is passed from death unto life" (John 5:24).

"By grace are ye saved through faith; and that not of yourselves: it is the gift of God: not of works, lest any man should boast" (Eph. 2:8, 9).

"So then faith cometh by hearing, and hearing by the Word of God" (Rom. 10:17).

"If thou shalt confess with thy mouth the Lord Jesus, and shalt believe in thine heart that God hath raised Him from the dead, thou shalt be saved. For with the heart man believeth unto righteousness; and with the mouth confession is made unto salvation" (Rom. 10:9, 10).